OSINT COMMANDO

PENETRATING NETWORKS WITH SPOKEO, SPIDERFOOT, SEON, AND LAMPYRE

4 BOOKS IN 1

BOOK 1
OSINT COMMANDO: A COMPREHENSIVE GUIDE FOR BEGINNERS AND EXPERTS

BOOK 2
FROM NOVICE TO NINJA: MASTERING OSINT COMMANDO WITH SPOKEO, SPIDERFOOT, SEON, AND LAMPYRE

BOOK 3
OSINT COMMANDO UNLEASHED: TAKING YOUR SKILLS FROM ENTRY-LEVEL TO ELITE

BOOK 4
EXPERT STRATEGIES IN OSINT COMMANDO: UNLOCKING SECRETS AT EVERY SKILL LEVEL

ROB BOTWRIGHT

Published by Rob Botwright
Library of Congress Cataloging-in-Publication Data
ISBN 978-1-83938-614-5
Cover design by Rizzo

Disclaimer

The contents of this book are based on extensive research and the best available historical sources. However, the author and publisher make no claims, promises, or guarantees about the accuracy, completeness, or adequacy of the information contained herein. The information in this book is provided on an "as is" basis, and the author and publisher disclaim any and all liability for any errors, omissions, or inaccuracies in the information or for any actions taken in reliance on such information. The opinions and views expressed in this book are those of the author and do not necessarily reflect the official policy or position of any organization or individual mentioned in this book. Any reference to specific people, places, or events is intended only to provide historical context and is not intended to defame or malign any group, individual, or entity. The information in this book is intended for educational and entertainment purposes only. It is not intended to be a substitute for professional advice or judgment. Readers are encouraged to conduct their own research and to seek professional advice where appropriate. Every effort has been made to obtain necessary permissions and acknowledgments for all images and other copyrighted material used in this book. Any errors or omissions in this regard are unintentional, and the author and publisher will correct them in future editions.

BOOK 1 - OSINT COMMANDO: A COMPREHENSIVE GUIDE FOR BEGINNERS AND EXPERTS

Introduction 5
Chapter 1: Introduction to OSINT and Its Applications 8
Chapter 2: Setting Up Your OSINT Toolkit 15
Chapter 3: Navigating the Spokeo Tool for Beginners 23
Chapter 4: Advanced Spokeo Techniques for Experts 29
Chapter 5: Spiderfoot: From Basics to Advanced Reconnaissance 36
Chapter 6: SEON: Harnessing Open-Source Intelligence for Beginners 44
Chapter 7: Lampyre: Advanced OSINT Investigations 52
Chapter 8: Data Analysis and Visualization for OSINT Professionals 60
Chapter 9: Ethical Considerations and Legal Implications 70
Chapter 10: OSINT Case Studies and Real-World Scenarios 78

BOOK 2 - FROM NOVICE TO NINJA: MASTERING OSINT COMMANDO WITH SPOKEO, SPIDERFOOT, SEON, AND LAMPYRE

Chapter 1: Embracing the OSINT Journey 87
Chapter 2: Building a Solid Foundation in OSINT 94
Chapter 3: Spokeo Essentials for Novices 102
Chapter 4: Spokeo Mastery for OSINT Ninjas 109
Chapter 5: Unraveling Spiderfoot's Beginner Techniques 116
Chapter 6: Spiderfoot's Advanced Ninja Strategies 123
Chapter 7: SEON: A Novice's Guide to Open-Source Intelligence 131
Chapter 8: SEON Expertise: Advanced OSINT Tactics 137
Chapter 9: Lampyre Basics and Beyond 143
Chapter 10: Becoming an OSINT Ninja: Real-World Applications and Challenges 150

BOOK 3 - OSINT COMMANDO UNLEASHED: TAKING YOUR SKILLS FROM ENTRY-LEVEL TO ELITE

Chapter 1: The Journey Begins: Exploring the OSINT Landscape 159
Chapter 2: Building a Strong OSINT Foundation 167
Chapter 3: Spokeo: From Entry-Level Exploration to Elite Mastery 174
Chapter 4: Spiderfoot Unleashed: Advanced Techniques for OSINT Pros 181
Chapter 5: SEON: Elevating Your Skills to Elite Levels 189
Chapter 6: Lampyre: Advanced Tools and Techniques for Elite Commandos 197
Chapter 7: Data Analysis and Visualization for Elite OSINT Professionals 204
Chapter 8: Ethical Considerations and Legal Expertise 212
Chapter 9: Elite Commandos in Action: Real-World OSINT Scenarios 219
Chapter 10: Becoming an Elite OSINT Commando: Challenges and Achievements 226

BOOK 4 - EXPERT STRATEGIES IN OSINT COMMANDO: UNLOCKING SECRETS AT EVERY SKILL LEVEL

Chapter 1: The OSINT Commando Spectrum 233
Chapter 2: Mastering the Fundamentals: A Deep Dive 239
Chapter 3: Advanced Spokeo Techniques for Experts 246
Chapter 4: Spiderfoot Mastery: Expert-Level Reconnaissance 253
Chapter 5: SEON: Advanced Strategies for the Informed Expert 259
Chapter 6: Lampyre's Hidden Potentials: Expert Insights 265
Chapter 7: Data Analysis and Visualization: Expert Approaches 272
Chapter 8: Legal and Ethical Challenges for OSINT Experts 279
Chapter 9: Expert OSINT Case Studies and Challenges 286
Chapter 10: Achieving Mastery: Expert Commando Stories and Takeaways 293
Conclusion 299

Introduction

Welcome to the world of "OSINT Commando," a comprehensive book bundle that will take you on an exhilarating journey through the realm of Open-Source Intelligence (OSINT). In an age where information is power, mastering the art of OSINT is not only a valuable skill but also an essential one. Whether you are a beginner seeking to grasp the basics or an expert aiming to unlock the deepest secrets, this bundle has something to offer everyone.

The digital landscape is a vast and ever-evolving ecosystem, where information flows freely, and data trails are left behind by individuals, organizations, and entities of all kinds. OSINT is the key that unlocks this treasure trove of knowledge, enabling you to navigate the complexities of the digital world, gather critical intelligence, and make informed decisions.

Our four-part journey begins with "Book 1 - OSINT Commando: A Comprehensive Guide for Beginners and Experts." Here, we lay the foundation for your OSINT exploration, ensuring that you understand the core principles, ethics, and methodologies that underpin this fascinating field. Whether you are a novice taking your first steps or an experienced practitioner looking to refine your skills, this book offers insights and guidance for all levels of expertise.

"Book 2 - From Novice to Ninja: Mastering OSINT Commando with Spokeo, Spiderfoot, SEON, and Lampyre" takes you deeper into the world of OSINT. We delve into the capabilities of four powerful OSINT tools – Spokeo, Spiderfoot, SEON, and Lampyre. Through hands-on tutorials and real-world examples, we equip you with the skills to become an OSINT ninja, capable of harnessing these tools for advanced reconnaissance and intelligence gathering.

"Book 3 - OSINT Commando Unleashed: Taking Your Skills from Entry-Level to Elite" reveals the secrets of elite OSINT practitioners. We explore advanced techniques, strategies, and methodologies used by the best in the field. Real-world case studies and challenging scenarios will push you to elevate your skills to an elite level, allowing you to tackle even the most complex OSINT challenges.

Finally, "Book 4 - Expert Strategies in OSINT Commando: Unlocking Secrets at Every Skill Level" provides a masterclass in OSINT expertise. We share expert-level strategies, insights, and tactics that can unlock the most well-guarded secrets. Through a collection of expert case studies and experiences, you will gain the wisdom of those who have reached the pinnacle of OSINT excellence.

Throughout this journey, we emphasize the importance of ethical conduct, legal compliance, and responsible information gathering. OSINT is a powerful tool, and with great power comes great responsibility. We encourage you to use your newfound expertise for positive and ethical purposes, respecting privacy and following the law.

The world of OSINT is dynamic, ever-evolving, and filled with endless possibilities. We invite you to embark on this adventure with an open mind, a thirst for knowledge, and a commitment to ethical practice. Whether you are just beginning or seeking to reach the highest levels of expertise, the "OSINT Commando" book bundle is your trusted companion on this exciting journey.

So, gear up, sharpen your skills, and get ready to penetrate networks, uncover secrets, and become a true OSINT Commando. The digital frontier awaits your exploration, and the knowledge contained within these pages will be your guide.

BOOK 1
OSINT COMMANDO
A COMPREHENSIVE GUIDE FOR BEGINNERS AND EXPERTS

ROB BOTWRIGHT

Chapter 1: Introduction to OSINT and Its Applications

Understanding Open-Source Intelligence (OSINT) is crucial in today's digital age. OSINT is a methodology for collecting and analyzing information from publicly available sources, and it plays a significant role in various fields, including intelligence, law enforcement, cybersecurity, and even business intelligence. OSINT encompasses a wide range of data, such as news articles, social media posts, publicly accessible databases, and more, making it a valuable resource for uncovering insights and identifying trends.

OSINT is not limited to a single discipline; it combines elements of data collection, analysis, and critical thinking. It relies on the principles of open access to information, making it accessible to anyone with the skills and tools to harness its power. Whether you are a novice looking to get started or an expert seeking advanced techniques, OSINT offers a wealth of opportunities for exploration.

The core idea behind OSINT is to gather information from publicly available sources to generate intelligence and make informed decisions. This approach stands in contrast to other intelligence-gathering methods that rely on classified or confidential data. OSINT is often considered the first step in the intelligence cycle, providing a foundation upon which further analysis and investigation can build.

To become proficient in OSINT, one must understand the sources and techniques involved. OSINT sources include websites, social media platforms, public records, government publications, academic research, and more. These sources can yield a variety of data types, such as text, images, videos, and geospatial information. The key is to know where to look and how to extract relevant information effectively.

One of the fundamental aspects of OSINT is the utilization of specialized tools and software. These tools assist in automating data collection, parsing large datasets, and visualizing information. Spokeo, Spiderfoot, SEON, and Lampyre are just a few examples of OSINT tools that can aid in different aspects of the intelligence-gathering process.

Spokeo, for instance, is a comprehensive people search engine that allows users to search for individuals using various criteria like name, email address, or phone number. It can be valuable for identifying and verifying individuals, making it a valuable asset for OSINT investigations.

Spiderfoot, on the other hand, is a versatile reconnaissance tool that can automate the collection of information from a wide range of sources, including social networks, search engines, and DNS records. It can uncover relationships between data points, providing valuable context for OSINT analysts.

SEON specializes in the analysis of online content and social media, helping OSINT practitioners monitor and assess digital footprints and trends. It allows for real-time data collection and analysis, enabling rapid response to emerging situations.

Lampyre, meanwhile, excels in data analysis and visualization. It can handle large datasets, making it ideal for uncovering hidden patterns and relationships within OSINT data.

Mastering these tools requires dedicated training and practice, but they can significantly enhance the efficiency and effectiveness of OSINT operations. As you delve deeper into OSINT, you'll discover that the true power lies not only in the tools but also in the analytical skills and critical thinking you bring to the table.

Beyond tools and techniques, OSINT also involves a strong ethical component. Practitioners must operate within legal and ethical boundaries, respecting privacy and avoiding actions that could harm individuals or organizations. Ethical considerations are crucial in maintaining the integrity of OSINT practices and ensuring that information is used responsibly.

Legal constraints vary by jurisdiction, so it's essential to be aware of the laws and regulations governing OSINT activities in your area. This knowledge is especially vital for professionals working in intelligence, law enforcement, and corporate security, where compliance with legal requirements is paramount.

One of the distinguishing features of OSINT is its adaptability and relevance across a wide spectrum of disciplines. In the realm of cybersecurity, for example, OSINT can be used to identify vulnerabilities and assess potential threats by monitoring hacker forums and analyzing online chatter.

In the field of journalism, OSINT can aid in fact-checking and verifying information from various sources, helping journalists deliver accurate and reliable news to the public. Journalists can also employ OSINT to uncover hidden stories and expose wrongdoing.

Businesses can leverage OSINT to gather market intelligence, track competitors, and identify potential risks and opportunities. It can inform strategic decisions, assist in due diligence processes, and enhance brand reputation management.

For intelligence agencies and law enforcement, OSINT is an invaluable tool for tracking criminal activities, monitoring extremist groups, and identifying threats to national security. It complements traditional intelligence gathering and analysis by providing real-time data from open sources.

Moreover, OSINT has significant applications in disaster response and humanitarian efforts. By monitoring social media and online forums, organizations can gain insights into evolving crises, enabling faster and more targeted responses to emergencies.

As you embark on your journey into the world of OSINT, remember that it is an evolving field. New tools, techniques, and data sources emerge regularly, and staying up-to-date is essential. Additionally, networking and collaboration with other OSINT professionals can provide valuable insights and open doors to new opportunities.

In summary, OSINT is a versatile and dynamic discipline that empowers individuals and organizations to gather valuable intelligence from publicly available sources. Whether you are a beginner taking your first steps or an expert seeking to refine your skills, the world of OSINT offers a wealth of knowledge waiting to be explored. Embrace the journey, master the fundamentals, and unlock the secrets hidden in the open-source world.

Real-world applications of OSINT span across a multitude of fields and industries, showcasing its versatility and significance in today's information-driven world.

In the realm of national security and intelligence, OSINT plays a pivotal role in monitoring potential threats and gathering crucial information from open sources, including social media, news articles, and publicly accessible databases.

Law enforcement agencies utilize OSINT techniques to aid in investigations, locate missing persons, track criminal activities, and assess potential risks in various communities.

In the world of cybersecurity, OSINT is a vital tool for identifying vulnerabilities, tracking cyber threats, and monitoring hacker forums and online chatter to safeguard organizations from cyberattacks.

Journalists rely on OSINT to fact-check information, verify sources, and uncover hidden stories, helping ensure the accuracy and credibility of news reporting.

Businesses leverage OSINT to gather market intelligence, track competitors, and identify emerging trends, enabling informed decision-making and strategic planning.

In the corporate world, OSINT assists in due diligence processes, brand reputation management, and supply chain monitoring, reducing risks and enhancing overall business operations.

OSINT is increasingly used in disaster response and humanitarian efforts, enabling organizations to gain real-time insights into evolving crises by monitoring social media and online forums, thus facilitating more effective responses to emergencies.

Government agencies employ OSINT for various purposes, including tracking extremist groups, monitoring geopolitical developments, and analyzing public sentiment to inform policy decisions.

In the academic realm, OSINT supports research endeavors by providing access to publicly available data and facilitating data analysis and visualization.

Security professionals use OSINT to conduct threat assessments, assess physical security vulnerabilities, and gather information for protective intelligence measures.

For individuals, OSINT can be a valuable resource for personal security, online reputation management, and locating long-lost friends or family members.

OSINT also plays a role in humanitarian efforts by aiding in the identification of individuals affected by conflicts, disasters, or displacement, helping reconnect families and provide assistance to those in need.

Counter-terrorism units utilize OSINT to monitor the online activities of extremist groups, track recruitment efforts, and assess the threat landscape.

In the healthcare industry, OSINT can assist in monitoring public health trends, tracking disease outbreaks, and identifying potential health risks within communities.

For financial institutions, OSINT supports fraud detection and anti-money laundering efforts by providing insights into financial transactions and activities that may raise red flags.

OSINT is integral in monitoring geopolitical developments, assessing international relations, and analyzing public sentiment to inform foreign policy decisions.

In the field of competitive intelligence, OSINT aids in tracking competitors' activities, product launches, and market strategies, allowing businesses to adapt and stay competitive.

OSINT is invaluable for crisis management, providing real-time information during emergencies, such as natural disasters, terrorist incidents, or public health crises, enabling rapid response and resource allocation.

For the military, OSINT assists in assessing the capabilities and intentions of foreign adversaries, aiding in strategic planning and defense preparedness.

In the field of academia, researchers use OSINT to access publicly available data and conduct studies in various domains, from social sciences to geography and beyond.

Non-governmental organizations (NGOs) rely on OSINT to gather information on human rights violations, humanitarian crises, and environmental issues, facilitating advocacy and intervention efforts.

OSINT also supports due diligence in mergers and acquisitions, helping organizations assess potential risks and opportunities associated with investment decisions.

For investigative journalists, OSINT tools and techniques are instrumental in uncovering corruption, exposing fraud, and revealing hidden agendas, leading to impactful investigative reporting.

In the field of public relations, OSINT assists in monitoring public sentiment and tracking online mentions, enabling organizations to manage their reputations effectively.

Overall, OSINT is a versatile and indispensable tool in today's information age, offering a wide array of applications across diverse sectors and industries. Its ability to harness publicly available data from a multitude of sources empowers individuals and organizations to make informed decisions, respond to emerging challenges, and contribute to a more transparent and connected world.

Chapter 2: Setting Up Your OSINT Toolkit

In the world of Open-Source Intelligence (OSINT), selecting the right tools is paramount to success.

These tools enable OSINT practitioners to gather, analyze, and visualize information from publicly available sources effectively.

The choice of tools depends on the specific goals of the OSINT operation and the nature of the data being sought.

For beginners, it's essential to start with user-friendly and versatile tools that provide a solid foundation.

One such tool is Spokeo, a people search engine that allows users to search for individuals using various criteria like name, email address, or phone number.

Spokeo's intuitive interface makes it an excellent choice for those new to OSINT, as it simplifies the process of locating and verifying individuals.

As practitioners gain experience, they may want to explore more advanced tools like Spiderfoot, which automates the collection of information from a wide range of sources, including social networks, search engines, and DNS records.

Spiderfoot's extensive capabilities provide OSINT experts with a powerful resource for comprehensive investigations.

SEON, another valuable tool, specializes in the analysis of online content and social media.

It helps OSINT practitioners monitor digital footprints and trends, making it an essential tool for staying updated on the latest developments.

For those delving into data analysis, Lampyre is an excellent choice.

Lampyre excels in data analysis and visualization, making it ideal for uncovering hidden patterns and relationships within OSINT data.

Selecting the right mix of tools depends on one's specific needs and objectives.

Beginners may want to focus on mastering a few user-friendly tools before venturing into more complex OSINT operations.

As proficiency grows, the use of multiple tools in combination can yield more comprehensive results.

It's essential to keep in mind that OSINT is a dynamic field, and new tools emerge regularly.

Staying updated on the latest developments in OSINT technology can provide a competitive edge.

Additionally, some OSINT tools are open source, while others may require a subscription or purchase.

Understanding the costs associated with each tool is crucial when building an OSINT toolkit.

Furthermore, some OSINT tools offer integration with other software or platforms, allowing for seamless data transfer and analysis.

When selecting OSINT tools, it's essential to consider factors such as data accuracy, search capabilities, data visualization options, and user support.

User reviews and recommendations from fellow OSINT practitioners can also provide valuable insights into the effectiveness of different tools.

For individuals or organizations conducting OSINT on a larger scale, it may be worth investing in specialized software or custom solutions tailored to their needs.

While tools are a crucial component of OSINT, they are not the sole determinant of success.

The skills, techniques, and strategies employed by OSINT practitioners are equally important.

Proficiency in online search techniques, source evaluation, and data analysis is essential for extracting meaningful intelligence from open sources.

Moreover, critical thinking and the ability to connect disparate pieces of information are skills that set exceptional OSINT practitioners apart.

Ethical considerations also play a vital role in OSINT operations.

Respecting privacy and adhering to legal and ethical boundaries are paramount in maintaining the integrity of OSINT practices.

Understanding the laws and regulations governing OSINT activities in one's jurisdiction is essential.

Failure to comply with legal requirements can lead to severe consequences.

As such, OSINT practitioners must conduct their investigations responsibly and ethically.

The ever-evolving landscape of technology and online platforms means that OSINT practitioners must adapt continually.

New social media platforms, websites, and data sources emerge regularly, providing fresh opportunities for OSINT practitioners to uncover information.

However, it also means that OSINT professionals must stay vigilant and aware of potential changes in the online environment that may impact their investigations.

Additionally, OSINT practitioners should be aware of the risks associated with their activities.

Depending on the nature of the investigation, individuals or organizations may not take kindly to the gathering of information from open sources.

Cybersecurity precautions, such as using VPNs and secure communication channels, are essential for safeguarding against potential threats.

In summary, selecting essential OSINT tools is a critical step in the intelligence-gathering process.

The right combination of tools, combined with the right skills and ethical practices, can empower OSINT practitioners to uncover valuable insights and make informed decisions.

The dynamic nature of the OSINT field requires continuous learning and adaptation to stay effective in the ever-changing online landscape.

Ultimately, OSINT serves as a valuable resource for individuals and organizations seeking to gather intelligence from publicly available sources, contributing to informed decision-making and improved situational awareness.

Configuring your OSINT workspace is a crucial step in preparing for effective open-source intelligence (OSINT) operations.

A well-organized and optimized workspace can significantly enhance your productivity and efficiency during investigations.

To begin, select a dedicated and comfortable workspace where you can concentrate on your OSINT tasks without distractions.

Consider factors such as lighting, ergonomics, and noise levels to create an environment conducive to focused work.

Your choice of hardware is also essential when configuring your OSINT workspace.

Ensure that you have a reliable and up-to-date computer or laptop with sufficient processing power and memory to handle the demands of OSINT activities.

A fast and stable internet connection is equally important, as OSINT often involves accessing online sources and databases.

Consider using a virtual private network (VPN) to enhance your online security and privacy while conducting OSINT operations.

Operating system preferences vary, but many OSINT tools and applications are compatible with both Windows and Linux.

Select an operating system that you are comfortable with and that suits your specific OSINT requirements.

To optimize your OSINT workspace, invest in dual monitors if possible.

Having two screens allows you to multitask more efficiently, with one monitor dedicated to research and data collection while the other is used for analysis and visualization.

When it comes to software, create a list of essential OSINT tools and applications that you will need for your investigations.

This may include web browsers, data analysis software, and the OSINT tools discussed in previous chapters, such as Spokeo, Spiderfoot, SEON, and Lampyre.

Organize your software applications into folders or categories to streamline access and reduce clutter on your desktop.

Consider using a password manager to secure your login credentials for various OSINT platforms and tools.

A password manager helps you maintain strong, unique passwords for each account, enhancing security.

Ensure that your antivirus and firewall software are up-to-date and configured to provide robust protection against potential threats while conducting OSINT operations.

Organize your digital files and documents systematically within your workspace.

Create folders and subfolders for different projects or investigations to keep information well-structured and easily accessible.

Regularly back up your data to an external storage device or a cloud-based service to safeguard against data loss.

Maintain a record of your OSINT activities and findings by keeping a detailed log or journal.

Documenting your process and observations can be invaluable for future reference and reporting.

Consider using a dedicated notebook or digital note-taking software to keep track of your notes and findings.

Set up a dedicated email account for OSINT operations to separate your professional and personal communications.

This can help prevent confusion and maintain the security of your personal information.

Maintain a list of reliable and reputable OSINT sources, websites, and databases that you frequently access.

Having a curated list of sources can save you time and ensure that you consistently gather information from trusted outlets.

To optimize your OSINT workspace further, establish a routine for your investigations.

Allocate specific time slots for different tasks, such as data collection, analysis, and reporting.

Prioritize your tasks based on their urgency and importance to stay organized and focused.

Stay updated on the latest OSINT techniques and tools by regularly engaging with the OSINT community.

Participate in forums, online communities, and conferences to learn from others and share your knowledge.

Consider forming partnerships or collaborations with other OSINT practitioners to leverage their expertise and resources.

When configuring your OSINT workspace, pay attention to data security and privacy.

Use encryption tools and secure communication channels when handling sensitive information.

Adhere to ethical guidelines and legal regulations to ensure that your OSINT activities are conducted responsibly and within the boundaries of the law.

Incorporate privacy-enhancing measures into your workflow, such as using virtual machines or anonymizing your online presence when necessary.

Regularly update and patch your software applications and operating system to protect your workspace from vulnerabilities.

Implement strong access controls and password policies to prevent unauthorized access to your OSINT workspace.

Consider using a dedicated and isolated virtual environment for particularly sensitive investigations to minimize risks.

When it comes to physical security, ensure that your workspace is physically secure, especially if you work with confidential or sensitive information.

Use physical locks, access control systems, and surveillance measures if necessary.

Regularly assess and audit your OSINT workspace to identify and address any potential vulnerabilities or weaknesses.

Maintain a contingency plan for unexpected events or emergencies, such as data breaches or hardware failures.

Having backup systems and procedures in place can help you recover quickly and minimize disruptions to your OSINT operations.

In summary, configuring your OSINT workspace is a critical aspect of preparing for effective and efficient OSINT operations.

By optimizing your hardware, software, and workspace organization, you can enhance your productivity, security, and overall performance in the field of open-source intelligence.

Remember to prioritize data security, privacy, and ethical considerations in all your OSINT activities, and stay vigilant against potential risks and threats.
A well-configured OSINT workspace is a valuable asset that can empower you to uncover valuable insights and make informed decisions in the world of open-source intelligence.

Chapter 3: Navigating the Spokeo Tool for Beginners

The Spokeo interface is the gateway to a wealth of information and a powerful resource for open-source intelligence (OSINT) practitioners.

Upon accessing the Spokeo platform, users are greeted with a clean and user-friendly design, making it accessible to both beginners and experienced investigators.

The main dashboard provides a clear layout, featuring a search bar prominently at the top.

The search bar is where users input the criteria for their searches, such as a person's name, email address, phone number, or username.

Beneath the search bar, users can find options for refining their searches, such as location filters and category filters, allowing for more precise results.

Users can select specific categories like "People," "Phone," "Email," or "Username" to tailor their search to their specific needs.

Below the search options, users will find a "Search" button to initiate their query.

Once a search is initiated, Spokeo begins scanning its vast database to retrieve relevant information.

The search results are presented in an organized manner, with each result displayed as a card.

Each card typically includes a profile picture, name, age, location, and a brief summary of the person's details.

Clicking on a card provides access to more detailed information, such as contact details, social media profiles, associated people, and additional background data.

Spokeo also offers a feature called "Saved Searches," allowing users to store and revisit their previous queries conveniently.

The platform enables users to save and organize their findings, streamlining the investigation process.

Users can also set up alerts for specific individuals or criteria, receiving notifications when new information matching their criteria becomes available.

Spokeo offers a comprehensive search experience, allowing users to uncover a wide range of information about individuals.

The platform can provide details about a person's social media presence, including profiles on platforms like Facebook, Twitter, LinkedIn, and Instagram.

It can also reveal information about a person's relatives, associates, and contact details, such as email addresses and phone numbers.

Spokeo's database includes public records, which means users can access data related to addresses, property ownership, and criminal records when applicable.

Users can also find information related to an individual's education, employment history, and even details about their online interests and hobbies.

Spokeo provides a versatile and valuable resource for OSINT practitioners, offering a convenient way to gather information from publicly available sources.

The platform's ease of use and intuitive design make it accessible to individuals of varying skill levels.

Whether you are a beginner looking to verify a person's identity or an experienced investigator conducting in-depth research, Spokeo's interface provides the tools necessary to achieve your objectives.

One of the notable advantages of the Spokeo interface is its ability to aggregate information from various sources into a single, coherent profile.

This consolidation of data simplifies the investigative process by providing a comprehensive overview of an individual's online presence and background.

The Spokeo interface's organization of data into cards and profiles enhances the user's ability to absorb and analyze information efficiently.

Furthermore, the platform offers valuable data visualization features, such as maps displaying geographic information and graphs illustrating relationship connections.

These visual aids help users gain insights and context from the data they collect, aiding in the investigative process.

Spokeo's interface is also adaptable, allowing users to navigate through search results seamlessly and explore connections and associations between individuals.

The ability to view associated people and related profiles enables users to uncover potential connections and relationships.

In summary, the Spokeo interface serves as a valuable tool for OSINT practitioners, providing a user-friendly gateway to a vast database of publicly available information.

Its design, search options, data organization, and visualization features make it a versatile resource for conducting investigations, verifying identities, and uncovering insights about individuals.

Whether used by beginners or seasoned investigators, the Spokeo interface empowers users to gather valuable intelligence from open sources effectively and efficiently.

Basic searches and navigation are fundamental skills when using the Spokeo platform for open-source intelligence (OSINT) investigations. To begin, users can access the Spokeo website through a web browser and log in with their credentials.

Upon logging in, users are presented with the Spokeo dashboard, which serves as the central hub for their OSINT activities. In the search bar at the top of the dashboard, users can enter the criteria for their searches.

Common search criteria include a person's first and last name, email address, phone number, or username. Users can refine their searches further by selecting specific filters, such as location filters or category filters, to narrow down their results.

The category filters allow users to specify whether they are searching for people, phone numbers, email addresses, or usernames.

Once the search criteria are entered, users can click the "Search" button to initiate the query.

Spokeo then begins scanning its extensive database to retrieve relevant information based on the provided criteria.

The search results are displayed in an organized manner, with each result appearing as a card.

Each card typically includes a profile picture (if available), the person's full name, age, location, and a brief summary of their details.

Users can click on individual cards to access more detailed information about the person.

Clicking on a card opens a profile page, where users can explore a wealth of information related to the individual they are investigating.

The profile page provides contact details, including email addresses and phone numbers, when available.

Users can also find links to the person's social media profiles, allowing them to explore their online presence further.

Spokeo often includes information about a person's relatives and associates, providing context and potential connections.

Additionally, the platform may display public records related to the individual, such as addresses, property ownership details, and criminal records when applicable.

Users can navigate through search results by clicking on the pagination options at the bottom of the page or by using the arrow buttons to move between pages.

Spokeo's interface is designed to be user-friendly and intuitive, making it accessible to individuals of various skill levels.

The platform's search bar, filters, and search results are organized to provide a straightforward and efficient investigative experience.

Spokeo's simplicity extends to its menu options, which are easily accessible from the main dashboard.

Users can explore features like "Saved Searches," where they can store and revisit previous queries, streamlining their investigation process.

Saved Searches allow users to maintain an organized record of their findings and expedite future research.

Furthermore, users can set up "Alerts" to monitor specific individuals or criteria.

These alerts notify users when new information matching their specified criteria becomes available on the platform.

The ability to set up alerts ensures that OSINT practitioners stay informed about relevant developments.

Spokeo also offers a convenient "Help" section, which provides resources, guides, and frequently asked questions to assist users in navigating the platform effectively.

For beginners, this section can serve as a valuable reference for learning how to use Spokeo efficiently.

In summary, basic searches and navigation are fundamental aspects of using the Spokeo platform for OSINT investigations.

Users can initiate searches by entering criteria in the search bar and refining their queries with filters.

The search results are displayed as cards, with each card containing essential information about the person being investigated.

Users can click on cards to access more detailed profiles and explore contact details, social media links, relatives, associates, and public records.

The platform's user-friendly interface, saved searches, alerts, and help resources contribute to a seamless investigative experience.

Whether you are a beginner or an experienced OSINT practitioner, mastering basic searches and navigation in Spokeo is essential for gathering valuable intelligence from open sources effectively.

Chapter 4: Advanced Spokeo Techniques for Experts

In open-source intelligence (OSINT) investigations, advanced search filters and operators are essential tools for refining queries and obtaining specific and targeted information.

Spokeo offers a range of advanced search features that enable users to narrow down their searches and uncover more precise results.

One of the powerful features provided by Spokeo is the ability to use quotation marks to search for an exact phrase.

By placing a phrase within quotation marks, users can instruct Spokeo to search for that exact sequence of words, ensuring highly relevant results.

For example, entering "John Smith" in quotes will yield results containing that precise name, rather than separate results for "John" and "Smith."

Spokeo also allows users to use Boolean operators such as "AND," "OR," and "NOT" to further customize their searches.

The "AND" operator is used to narrow down results by requiring that all specified criteria are met.

For instance, searching for "John Smith" AND "New York" will only yield results that include both the name "John Smith" and the location "New York."

Conversely, the "OR" operator broadens results by including any of the specified criteria.

Searching for "John Smith" OR "Jane Smith" will retrieve results for both individuals.

The "NOT" operator is employed to exclude specific criteria from the search results.

A query like "John Smith" NOT "New York" will exclude any results associated with "John Smith" in New York.

To further refine searches, Spokeo allows users to use wildcards, represented by asterisks (*), to substitute for unknown characters in a search term.

For example, searching for "J*n Sm*th" will retrieve results for variations like "John Smith" and "Janet Smyth."

Users can also use parentheses to group criteria and control the order of operations in complex queries.

For instance, "(John OR Jane) AND Smith" ensures that the search prioritizes results for individuals named "John Smith" and "Jane Smith."

Spokeo offers category-specific filters that allow users to narrow down results by specific criteria related to different categories.

For instance, in the "People" category, users can filter by age, location, relatives, and associates.

In the "Phone" category, filters include phone type (mobile or landline) and carrier.

The "Email" category offers filters like email provider and domain.

In the "Username" category, users can filter by platform or website.

These category-specific filters provide a granular level of control over search results.

Users can also utilize location filters to target specific geographic areas, which can be particularly useful in OSINT investigations with regional considerations.

Spokeo offers location filters for countries, states, cities, and ZIP codes, enabling users to focus their searches on particular regions.

Moreover, the platform provides date of birth (DOB) filters that allow users to specify age ranges when searching for individuals.

These filters help users identify individuals within specific age groups, which can be crucial in investigations involving age-related criteria.

Spokeo's interface allows users to sort search results based on relevance, name, or age.

Sorting by relevance ensures that the most pertinent results appear at the top of the list, making it easier to identify the most relevant information quickly.

Users can also adjust the number of results displayed per page to suit their preferences, from a compact view to a more detailed view.

Spokeo's search history feature keeps track of previous queries, allowing users to revisit and re-run past searches conveniently.

This feature is especially useful for users who frequently revisit the same investigations or need to track changes in information over time.

Additionally, Spokeo offers a "Saved Searches" feature, allowing users to store and organize their most important or frequently used queries.

This feature streamlines the research process, enabling users to quickly access and rerun saved searches without entering criteria repeatedly.

In summary, advanced search filters and operators are indispensable tools in OSINT investigations using the Spokeo platform.

These features enable users to refine their queries, specify search criteria, and obtain highly targeted information.

The ability to use quotation marks, Boolean operators, wildcards, and parentheses empowers users to construct complex and precise queries.

Category-specific filters, location filters, DOB filters, and sorting options enhance the granularity of search control.

The search history and saved searches features contribute to efficient and organized investigations.

Mastering these advanced search capabilities in Spokeo is crucial for OSINT practitioners seeking to uncover valuable intelligence from open sources effectively.

Unlocking the full potential of Spokeo for open-source intelligence (OSINT) investigations involves not only mastering basic and advanced search techniques but also utilizing some of the platform's hidden features.

These features can provide valuable insights and enhance the efficiency of your investigations.

One such hidden feature is the ability to search for email addresses associated with a specific domain.

While Spokeo primarily focuses on searching for individuals, it can also help you identify email addresses linked to a particular organization or domain.

By entering the domain name (e.g., "@company.com") in the search bar, you can uncover a list of email addresses connected to that domain.

This can be especially useful when researching an organization's personnel or identifying potential points of contact.

Another hidden feature in Spokeo is the ability to track phone numbers and their history.

Spokeo allows users to search for phone numbers and provides information about the carrier, location, and sometimes even the owner's name.

Additionally, Spokeo can help you track the history of a phone number, revealing changes in ownership or usage over time.

This feature can be valuable in tracking individuals who may have changed their phone numbers to evade detection.

Spokeo also offers a reverse address lookup feature, allowing users to search for information about a specific address.

By entering an address in the search bar, you can access details such as property ownership, residents, and any associated phone numbers.

This feature can assist in identifying individuals living at a particular location or uncovering potential connections.

Spokeo's reverse username lookup is another hidden feature that can be beneficial in OSINT investigations.

By entering a username or online alias in the search bar, you can discover information about the person behind that username.

This feature can be useful in uncovering an individual's online presence and connecting it to their real-world identity.

Additionally, Spokeo offers a social media profile search capability.

By entering a person's name, you can access their social media profiles, including links to platforms like Facebook, Twitter, LinkedIn, and Instagram.

This feature allows you to explore an individual's online activity and connections across various social networks.

Furthermore, Spokeo provides insights into an individual's online interests and hobbies.

By analyzing the data available on an individual's profile, you can gain a better understanding of their preferences, activities, and affiliations.

This information can be valuable in building a comprehensive profile of the person you are investigating.

Spokeo also allows users to set up alerts for specific individuals or criteria.

By creating alerts, you can receive notifications when new information matching your specified criteria becomes available on the platform.

This feature ensures that you stay updated on relevant developments and changes related to your investigations.

Additionally, Spokeo offers a feature called "Research Central," which provides access to a variety of research tools and resources.

Here, you can find links to public records, background checks, and other useful tools that can complement your OSINT investigations.

Spokeo's "Help" section contains valuable resources, guides, and frequently asked questions to assist users in navigating the platform effectively.

This section can serve as a reference for learning how to use Spokeo's hidden features efficiently.

Users can also access Spokeo's blog, where they can find articles, tips, and insights related to OSINT and online investigations.

Engaging with the Spokeo community by participating in forums and discussions can provide opportunities to learn from others, share knowledge, and exchange ideas.

In summary, Spokeo offers several hidden features that can significantly enhance your OSINT investigations.

These features include searching for email addresses associated with a specific domain, tracking phone numbers and their history, performing reverse address and username lookups, and accessing social media profiles and online interests.

Setting up alerts, utilizing "Research Central," and exploring the "Help" section can further streamline your investigative process.

Engaging with the Spokeo community and staying informed through the platform's blog can contribute to your growth as an OSINT practitioner.

By leveraging these hidden features, you can uncover valuable intelligence from open sources effectively and efficiently.

Chapter 5: Spiderfoot: From Basics to Advanced Reconnaissance

Getting started with Spiderfoot is the first step toward harnessing its powerful capabilities for open-source intelligence (OSINT) investigations.

Spiderfoot is an OSINT automation tool designed to assist in the collection and analysis of information from various sources on the internet.

Before diving into the advanced features of Spiderfoot, it's essential to understand the basics and establish a strong foundation.

To begin, you'll need to download and install Spiderfoot on your computer or server.

Spiderfoot is an open-source tool, which means it's freely available for download and use.

Once you have Spiderfoot installed, you can access its web-based interface through a web browser.

The web interface provides an intuitive and user-friendly environment for conducting OSINT operations.

Before running your first scan, take some time to configure Spiderfoot to meet your specific needs and objectives.

Spiderfoot allows you to customize various settings, such as scan depth, scan speed, and data retention policies.

These settings will influence the scope and efficiency of your OSINT scans.

Spiderfoot also offers a range of modules that enable you to gather specific types of information.

Modules are essentially plugins that extend Spiderfoot's functionality and allow you to target different data sources.

For example, there are modules for collecting email addresses, domain information, social media profiles, and more.

Familiarize yourself with the available modules and choose the ones that align with your investigation's goals.

Once you've configured Spiderfoot and selected the appropriate modules, it's time to create your first scan profile.

A scan profile is a set of parameters that define the scope and targets of your OSINT operation.

You can specify the starting point for your scan, such as a domain name or IP address, and define any additional targets or exclusions.

Spiderfoot also allows you to set up authentication credentials for certain modules, ensuring that you can access restricted data sources.

When creating a scan profile, consider the specific information you want to gather and the sources where it is likely to be found.

Once your scan profile is set up, you can start the scan process.

Spiderfoot will begin collecting information from the sources specified in your modules and scan profile.

The progress of your scan will be displayed in the web interface, allowing you to monitor its status in real time.

As the scan progresses, Spiderfoot will compile the collected data into a comprehensive report.

The report will provide detailed information about the targets you specified in your scan profile, including their associated data and connections.

Spiderfoot's reporting feature is a valuable asset for OSINT practitioners, as it simplifies the process of analyzing and interpreting the gathered information.

The information in the report can be visualized using charts and graphs, making it easier to identify patterns, relationships, and potential leads.

Spiderfoot also offers export options, allowing you to save the results in various formats for further analysis or reporting.

In addition to its basic functionality, Spiderfoot provides several advanced features that can enhance your OSINT investigations.

One such feature is the ability to schedule scans, enabling you to automate recurring OSINT operations.

Scheduling scans can be particularly useful for monitoring specific targets or collecting regular updates on your subjects of interest.

Another advanced feature is the integration of third-party data sources and APIs.

Spiderfoot allows you to connect external data sources to enrich your OSINT scans further.

This integration can provide access to additional information and enhance the depth of your investigations.

Spiderfoot also offers the capability to set up alerts and notifications.

You can configure alerts to notify you when specific conditions are met during a scan, such as the discovery of certain keywords or changes in a target's online presence.

These alerts can help you stay informed and respond promptly to relevant developments.

Furthermore, Spiderfoot supports the use of custom scripts and plugins.

If you have specific requirements or want to extend Spiderfoot's functionality, you can develop custom scripts or plugins to tailor the tool to your needs.

These scripts can be used to interact with external APIs, manipulate data, or perform specialized tasks.

It's important to note that while Spiderfoot is a powerful OSINT tool, it is not a silver bullet.

Successful OSINT investigations require a combination of tools, techniques, and critical thinking.

Spiderfoot is most effective when used in conjunction with other OSINT resources and methodologies.

Additionally, ethical considerations and legal compliance are essential aspects of OSINT investigations.

Always conduct your investigations responsibly and within the boundaries of the law and ethical guidelines.

In summary, getting started with Spiderfoot is a crucial step in harnessing its capabilities for OSINT investigations.

Begin by downloading and configuring the tool, selecting the appropriate modules, and creating scan profiles that align with your objectives.

Monitor the progress of your scans and analyze the generated reports to extract valuable insights.

Explore advanced features such as scheduling scans, integrating external data sources, setting up alerts, and utilizing custom scripts to enhance your OSINT operations.

Remember that Spiderfoot is a valuable addition to your OSINT toolkit but should be used in conjunction with other resources and with a strong commitment to ethical and legal standards.

A deep dive into Spiderfoot modules is essential for understanding how to maximize the capabilities of this versatile open-source intelligence (OSINT) tool.

Modules are the heart of Spiderfoot's functionality, allowing users to target specific data sources and gather precise information.

One of the core modules in Spiderfoot is the "Domains to IPs" module, which enables users to discover the IP addresses associated with a given domain name.

This module can be valuable in OSINT investigations, as it helps identify the web servers and hosting infrastructure associated with a target domain.

Another fundamental module is the "IP Address to Domains" module, which performs the reverse of the previous module. It allows users to find domain names that resolve to a specified IP address, shedding light on potentially related websites or services.

The "Email Addresses" module is essential for uncovering email addresses associated with a target.

This module can help identify contact points, communication channels, and potential targets for further investigation.

The "Subdomains" module provides insights into the subdomains associated with a given domain name.

Understanding subdomains can reveal additional web assets and expand the scope of an OSINT investigation.

Social media plays a significant role in today's online landscape, making the "Social Media Profiles" module crucial.

This module searches for profiles on popular social media platforms, allowing users to gain insights into an individual's online presence and connections.

The "Publications" module focuses on identifying articles, papers, or publications associated with a target.

It can be particularly useful in academic or professional investigations to uncover an individual's work or contributions.

The "APIs" module offers the ability to connect with external data sources and APIs to gather supplemental information.

Integrating third-party data sources can enhance the depth and accuracy of OSINT investigations.

"Host Info" is a module that retrieves information about a target's web server, including the hosting provider, location, and other relevant details.

Understanding the infrastructure behind a target's online presence can be valuable for assessing potential vulnerabilities or dependencies.

The "Network Blocks" module provides information about IP address ranges associated with a target's organization.

This module is useful for gaining insights into an organization's network infrastructure and potential attack surfaces.

The "AS Number to Organization" module associates an Autonomous System (AS) number with the organization or entity that owns it.

This can be helpful in identifying the ownership and affiliations of network infrastructure.

In-depth analysis of domain registrations can be performed using the "Whois Records" module.

This module uncovers information about domain registrants, registration dates, and contact details, providing valuable context for an investigation.

The "Passive DNS" module offers historical data on DNS resolutions associated with a target domain.

This can reveal changes in infrastructure and online activities over time.

When it comes to email, the "Emails from Website" module extracts email addresses found on a target's website.

This module can be particularly useful for contact discovery and communication channels.

The "IP Neighbours" module identifies other IP addresses sharing the same network as a target.

Understanding the network neighborhood can provide insights into potential connections or associations.

The "Scanning IPs" module scans IP addresses for open ports and services, helping assess the security posture of a target's infrastructure.

In OSINT investigations, it's essential to consider the potential attack surface.

The "Open Ports" module complements the previous one by specifically focusing on open ports on a target's IP addresses. Identifying open ports can highlight potential vulnerabilities and services that might be of interest.

The "Leaked Credentials" module checks email addresses for appearances in publicly available databases of leaked credentials.

This module helps identify compromised accounts and potential security risks.

Understanding a target's online footprint often involves investigating its online infrastructure using the "DNS Records" module.

This module provides details about DNS records associated with a domain, such as MX records, TXT records, and more.

The "Cookies" module extracts and analyzes cookies used by a target's website, offering insights into user tracking and behavior.

Understanding cookie usage can be essential for privacy and security assessments.

In OSINT investigations, it's crucial to consider the potential online threats associated with a target.

The "Google Search" module performs automated Google searches for specific keywords or phrases related to the target.

This module can help uncover publicly available information and potential threats or risks.

The "File Metadata" module analyzes files associated with a target, extracting metadata such as author information, timestamps, and document properties.

This module can be valuable for understanding the origin and history of files linked to a target.

The "Leaked Documents" module searches for documents associated with a target that may have been publicly disclosed or leaked.

This module can reveal sensitive information and potential security issues.

In summary, Spiderfoot modules are essential components of the tool's functionality, allowing users to target specific data sources and gather precise information.

Each module serves a distinct purpose, enabling OSINT practitioners to tailor their investigations to their objectives.

Understanding how to use these modules effectively is key to maximizing the capabilities of Spiderfoot and obtaining valuable insights from open sources.

Chapter 6: SEON: Harnessing Open-Source Intelligence for Beginners

SEON, an open-source intelligence (OSINT) tool, offers powerful capabilities for collecting and analyzing data from various online sources, and to make the most of SEON, it's crucial to understand its setup and configuration.

Before you dive into using SEON, you need to ensure that you have it properly installed on your system.

SEON is available for Linux, and you can install it using package managers like APT or by downloading the source code from the official repository.

Once installed, you can start SEON and access its web-based interface through your preferred web browser.

The first step in setting up SEON is configuring its settings to align with your specific needs and preferences.

SEON offers a configuration file where you can define parameters such as the port it listens on, proxy settings, and logging preferences.

Take some time to review and modify these settings to ensure SEON operates optimally for your OSINT investigations.

SEON is highly modular, and its functionality is extended through plugins.

Before you start using SEON, it's essential to select the plugins that are relevant to your investigation objectives.

These plugins allow you to gather specific types of data from various online sources.

Some common plugin categories include social media, search engines, and website data.

To configure plugins, you need to access the "Settings" section within SEON's web interface.

Here, you can enable or disable plugins, specify API keys for some, and configure options such as request rate limits.

Consider your investigation's focus and the type of information you need to collect when configuring plugins.

A key aspect of SEON's setup is the creation of a project.

Projects are containers that organize your investigations and allow you to manage different cases or targets separately.

When setting up a project, you can specify its name, description, and the plugins that will be used for that particular investigation.

Projects help you keep your OSINT activities organized and maintain a clear separation between different cases or targets.

Once you've configured your plugins and set up a project, you can start creating tasks.

Tasks in SEON define what specific data you want to collect and from which sources.

Each task corresponds to a single query that SEON will execute to retrieve information.

Tasks can be created within a project, and you can specify parameters such as keywords, domains, or usernames.

You can also define search engines or social media platforms to target in your tasks.

SEON allows you to schedule tasks, so they can run automatically at specified intervals.

This automation feature is particularly useful for ongoing monitoring or data collection that needs to be repeated regularly.

To schedule tasks, navigate to the "Task Scheduler" section within SEON's web interface, and configure the frequency and timing of your tasks.

SEON offers a robust system for managing and organizing data.

Once your tasks have run and collected information, SEON stores the results in a structured manner.

You can access the collected data through the "Data Manager" section in the web interface.

Here, you can filter, sort, and search for specific information, making it easier to analyze and work with the data.

SEON also provides the option to export data in various formats, allowing you to share or further process the results.

In addition to data management, SEON offers a "Reporting" feature that allows you to generate reports based on the collected information.

Reports can be customized to include specific data points, and you can export them in formats such as PDF or HTML.

Customizing reports allows you to present findings in a clear and organized manner, which can be valuable for communication or documentation purposes.

Security is a crucial aspect of any OSINT investigation, and SEON provides options to enhance the security of your setup.

One important consideration is enabling authentication for access to SEON's web interface.

By setting up authentication, you can restrict access to authorized users, ensuring that sensitive data and investigations remain protected.

Authentication settings can be configured in the "Settings" section, under the "Authentication" tab.

Additionally, you can configure SEON to use a proxy server for outgoing requests.

This can help anonymize your activities and protect your identity during OSINT investigations.

Proxy settings can be adjusted in the "Settings" section, under the "Proxy" tab.

Monitoring and maintaining your SEON setup is essential for ensuring its effectiveness and reliability.

SEON offers logging capabilities that allow you to keep track of activities and troubleshoot any issues that may arise.

Logs can be accessed in the "Logs" section of the web interface, and you can customize logging levels and retention periods to suit your needs.

Regularly reviewing logs can help you identify any anomalies or potential security concerns.

Finally, staying informed about SEON updates and improvements is crucial for keeping your OSINT toolset up to date.

SEON is an actively developed tool, and updates may include bug fixes, new features, or improved plugin support.

By regularly checking for updates and following the official SEON repository, you can ensure that your installation remains current and capable of handling evolving OSINT challenges.

In summary, setting up and configuring SEON is a crucial step in harnessing its power for your OSINT investigations.

Proper installation, configuration of settings, selection of relevant plugins, and organization through projects are foundational aspects of SEON setup.

Creating and scheduling tasks, managing collected data, and generating reports are essential for conducting effective investigations.

Security considerations, such as enabling authentication and using proxy servers, help protect your identity and data.

Regular monitoring and keeping SEON up to date ensure its continued functionality and effectiveness in the ever-evolving landscape of open-source intelligence.

Embarking on beginner-level SEON investigations is an exciting journey into the world of open-source intelligence, and it's essential to start with a strong foundation to make the most of this powerful tool.

As a beginner, it's crucial to familiarize yourself with the basic concepts and interface of SEON.

The web-based interface of SEON is user-friendly and intuitive, making it accessible even for those with minimal technical expertise.

When you first access SEON, take some time to explore its layout and various sections to get a sense of how the tool is organized.

Before diving into your first investigation, you need to set up SEON and configure it to align with your specific needs and preferences.

Ensure that you have SEON properly installed on your system, and review the configuration settings to tailor them to your requirements.

The configuration settings in SEON allow you to specify parameters such as the port it listens on, proxy settings, and logging preferences.

These settings influence the tool's behavior and performance, so it's essential to adjust them accordingly.

Once you've configured SEON, it's time to select the plugins that are relevant to your beginner-level investigation.

SEON's strength lies in its modular design, with plugins extending its functionality to target specific data sources.

Take the time to review the available plugins and choose the ones that align with your investigation objectives.

Common plugin categories include social media, search engines, and website data.

Consider the type of information you aim to collect and which plugins are most suitable for your goals.

Creating a project is the next step in preparing for your SEON investigation.

Projects in SEON serve as containers that help you organize your investigations and manage different cases or targets separately. When setting up a project, you can specify its name, description, and the plugins that will be used for that particular investigation.

Projects provide structure and help you keep your OSINT activities organized. With SEON properly configured and plugins selected, it's time to create your first task. Tasks in SEON define what specific data you want to collect and from which sources. Each task corresponds to a single query that SEON will execute to retrieve information. Tasks can be created within a project, and you can specify parameters such as keywords, domains, or usernames.

You can also define the search engines or social media platforms to target in your tasks.

Consider the focus of your beginner-level investigation when creating tasks and select parameters that align with your objectives. SEON's automation capabilities allow you to schedule tasks to run automatically at specified intervals.

This automation feature is particularly useful for ongoing monitoring or data collection that needs to be repeated regularly.

To schedule tasks, navigate to the "Task Scheduler" section within SEON's web interface and configure the frequency and timing of your tasks.

Scheduling tasks can help you save time and maintain continuous monitoring of your targets.

Once your tasks have been scheduled, you can monitor their progress and access the collected data through SEON's web interface.

SEON stores the results in a structured manner, making it easier for you to filter, sort, and search for specific information.

The ability to manage and organize data effectively is crucial for any OSINT investigation, including beginner-level ones.

SEON offers export options that allow you to save the collected data in various formats for further analysis or reporting.

In addition to data management, SEON provides a "Reporting" feature that enables you to generate reports based on the collected information.

Reports can be customized to include specific data points, and you can export them in formats such as PDF or HTML.

Customizing reports allows you to present your findings in a clear and organized manner.

Security is an important consideration for beginner-level SEON investigations.

Ensure that you enable authentication for access to SEON's web interface.

Authentication settings can be configured in the "Settings" section under the "Authentication" tab.

By setting up authentication, you restrict access to authorized users, safeguarding sensitive data and investigations.

To enhance security further, you can configure SEON to use a proxy server for outgoing requests.

Proxy settings can be adjusted in the "Settings" section under the "Proxy" tab.

Using proxy servers can help anonymize your activities and protect your identity during OSINT investigations.

Monitoring and maintaining your SEON setup are vital to ensuring its effectiveness and reliability.

SEON offers logging capabilities that allow you to keep track of activities and troubleshoot any issues that may arise.

Regularly reviewing logs can help you identify anomalies or potential security concerns.

Staying informed about SEON updates and improvements is essential for keeping your OSINT toolset up to date.

SEON is actively developed, and updates may include bug fixes, new features, or improved plugin support.

By regularly checking for updates and following the official SEON repository, you ensure that your installation remains current and capable of handling evolving OSINT challenges.

Beginner-level SEON investigations are an excellent starting point for those new to open-source intelligence.

With the right foundation, configuration, and understanding of SEON's capabilities, you can begin your journey into the world of OSINT.

Remember to choose relevant plugins, create projects, and schedule tasks that align with your investigation objectives.

SEON's data management, reporting, and security features will support your beginner-level investigations and help you build a solid skillset in the field of open-source intelligence.

Chapter 7: Lampyre: Advanced OSINT Investigations

Exploring the Lampyre interface and its configuration is a crucial step in harnessing the capabilities of this open-source intelligence (OSINT) tool for your investigations.

Lampyre offers a user-friendly interface designed to facilitate data collection and analysis from various online sources.

Before you begin using Lampyre, it's essential to ensure that you have it correctly installed on your system.

Lampyre is available for Windows and can be easily downloaded and installed from the official website.

Once installed, you can launch Lampyre and access its interface, which is divided into different sections to help you navigate and organize your OSINT activities.

To get started, you need to understand the basic layout of the Lampyre interface.

The central area of the interface is the workspace, where you'll perform your OSINT tasks and create visual representations of your investigations.

The left sidebar provides access to various tools and modules, while the top menu contains additional options and settings.

Before diving into your first investigation, it's essential to configure Lampyre to align with your specific needs and preferences.

Lampyre's configuration settings allow you to customize the tool to operate optimally for your OSINT activities.

You can access the configuration settings by clicking on the gear icon in the top right corner of the interface.

Here, you can specify parameters such as proxy settings, user interface preferences, and data storage locations.

Take the time to review and adjust these settings to match your requirements.

Now that Lampyre is properly configured, it's time to explore the available modules and tools.

Lampyre offers a wide range of modules that extend its functionality, allowing you to collect and analyze data from diverse sources.

Modules are categorized based on their specific functions, such as data collection, transformation, analysis, and visualization.

To access the modules, click on the "Modules" tab in the left sidebar, and you'll see a list of available modules organized by categories.

Each module serves a particular purpose, and you can select and customize them according to your investigation goals.

To start using a module, simply drag it from the left sidebar and drop it into the workspace area.

Once a module is added to your workspace, you can configure its settings and parameters to tailor it to your specific needs.

The configuration options for each module may vary, but they typically include input fields, filters, and output settings.

Understanding how to use and configure these modules is essential for conducting effective OSINT investigations with Lampyre.

Now that you've configured your modules, it's time to create your first investigation.

An investigation in Lampyre is essentially a visual representation of your OSINT activities.

To create an investigation, click on the "Investigations" tab in the left sidebar, and then click the "+ New Investigation" button.

Give your investigation a name and description to help you stay organized and keep track of its purpose.

Once your investigation is created, you can start adding modules and connecting them to build your data collection and analysis workflow.

Lampyre offers a drag-and-drop interface that makes it easy to connect modules and visualize the flow of data in your investigation.

To connect modules, simply drag a line from the output of one module to the input of another.

This visual representation allows you to see how data flows between modules and helps you design effective investigation workflows.

As you add and configure modules in your investigation, you can monitor the progress and view the results in real time.

Lampyre provides a visual output for each module, making it easy to see the data collected and the transformations applied.

You can also access detailed information and logs for each module to troubleshoot and refine your investigation.

In addition to module-based data collection and analysis, Lampyre offers powerful data visualization capabilities.

The tool allows you to create interactive charts, graphs, and visual representations of your findings.

This visualization feature is valuable for summarizing complex data, identifying patterns, and presenting your discoveries effectively.

To create visualizations, you can use the built-in charting modules or export data to external visualization tools.

As you progress in your Lampyre investigations, you may want to save and organize your work.

Lampyre allows you to save your investigations as projects, making it easy to revisit and continue your research later.

Projects store all the modules, configurations, and data related to a specific investigation, ensuring that you can pick up where you left off.

To save your investigation as a project, click on the "File" menu and select "Save Project."

Give your project a meaningful name and description, and it will be available for future access.

Security considerations are essential when using Lampyre for OSINT investigations.

Ensure that you use Lampyre responsibly and ethically, and be aware of legal and ethical guidelines when conducting online research.

Lampyre is a powerful tool, and its capabilities can be used for both legitimate research and malicious activities.

To protect your privacy and security, consider using a virtual private network (VPN) when using Lampyre, especially if you are accessing sensitive or restricted data sources.

Additionally, always respect the terms of service and policies of the websites and online platforms you interact with during your investigations.

In summary, understanding the Lampyre interface and its configuration options is vital for successful OSINT investigations.

Proper installation, configuration, and module selection are essential to harness the full potential of this versatile tool.

Creating and organizing investigations, configuring modules, and visualizing data are key components of Lampyre's functionality.

Remember to use Lampyre responsibly and ethically, and stay informed about legal and ethical considerations in your OSINT activities.

With the right knowledge and skills, Lampyre can become a valuable asset in your open-source intelligence toolkit.

Mastering advanced data analysis with Lampyre opens up new dimensions of insight and capability in the realm of open-source intelligence (OSINT).

With a solid foundation in Lampyre's interface and configuration, you can delve into the world of complex data analysis and uncover valuable information.

To embark on advanced data analysis, it's crucial to understand the variety of data sources and types that Lampyre can handle.

Lampyre supports data from social media platforms, websites, documents, and more, making it a versatile tool for OSINT professionals.

One of the first steps in advanced data analysis is gathering data from multiple sources.

Lampyre's modular design allows you to create complex workflows that combine various modules to collect data comprehensively.

For example, you can create a workflow that starts with web scraping to collect website data, followed by social media scraping to gather information from different platforms.

The ability to orchestrate these modules and build custom data collection pipelines is a hallmark of advanced analysis with Lampyre.

Once you have collected data from multiple sources, you can move on to data integration and transformation.

Lampyre offers modules for data manipulation, cleansing, and merging, allowing you to prepare your data for in-depth analysis.

You can aggregate, filter, and structure your data to create a unified dataset that is ready for advanced analytical techniques.

Lampyre's data transformation capabilities are essential for ensuring that your analysis is based on high-quality and well-prepared data.

Advanced data analysis often involves statistical techniques and machine learning.

Lampyre provides integration with Python, enabling you to leverage powerful libraries such as NumPy, Pandas, and scikit-learn for statistical analysis and machine learning.

You can use Python scripts within Lampyre to perform advanced statistical tests, cluster data, or build predictive models.

This integration empowers you to explore complex data relationships and make data-driven predictions.

Furthermore, Lampyre's data visualization capabilities play a pivotal role in advanced analysis.

Visualizing your data can reveal patterns, trends, and anomalies that might not be apparent in raw numbers.

You can create interactive charts, graphs, and heatmaps to convey insights effectively to stakeholders or colleagues.

Lampyre's visualization modules make it easy to generate informative and visually appealing reports.

Time-series analysis is a valuable technique for understanding how data changes over time.

Lampyre offers tools for time-series analysis, enabling you to identify trends, seasonality, and other temporal patterns in your data.

You can visualize time-series data, apply smoothing techniques, and forecast future values using Lampyre's capabilities.

Time-series analysis is particularly useful when dealing with data that has a chronological component, such as social media posts or website traffic.

Sentiment analysis is another advanced analytical technique that Lampyre supports.

You can use natural language processing (NLP) modules to analyze text data, such as social media comments or news articles, and determine sentiment.

Sentiment analysis can help you gauge public opinion, detect emerging trends, or assess the impact of events on a particular topic.

Network analysis is a powerful approach for exploring relationships and connections within data.

Lampyre offers network analysis modules that allow you to create, visualize, and analyze networks or graphs.

You can uncover hidden relationships, identify central nodes, and assess network structures within your data.

Network analysis is invaluable for understanding social networks, communication patterns, or any dataset with interconnected elements.

In advanced data analysis, data enrichment is a crucial step.

Lampyre offers modules for data enrichment that allow you to augment your dataset with additional information from external sources.

You can enrich your data with demographic data, geospatial information, or other relevant attributes to gain a more comprehensive understanding.

Data enrichment enhances the depth and context of your analysis.

Geospatial analysis is essential when dealing with location-based data.

Lampyre provides geospatial modules for mapping and analyzing data with geographic components.

You can visualize data on maps, perform spatial queries, and uncover geographic patterns or insights.

Geospatial analysis is particularly valuable in OSINT investigations involving physical locations or events.

As you delve deeper into advanced data analysis with Lampyre, you'll encounter the need for custom scripting and automation.

Lampyre's integration with Python allows you to develop custom scripts and workflows tailored to your specific analytical requirements.

You can automate repetitive tasks, create custom data transformations, and implement complex algorithms using Python within Lampyre.

This flexibility empowers you to tackle advanced analytical challenges effectively.

Ethical considerations remain paramount in advanced data analysis.

Ensure that your analysis adheres to legal and ethical guidelines, especially when dealing with sensitive or private data.

Respect privacy regulations, obtain necessary permissions, and anonymize data as needed to protect individuals' rights.

In summary, advanced data analysis with Lampyre represents a significant leap in your OSINT capabilities.

By mastering data collection, integration, transformation, statistical analysis, machine learning, visualization, and specialized techniques, you can uncover valuable insights and make informed decisions.

Lampyre's integration with Python, support for various data types, and versatile modules make it a powerful tool for advanced data analysis in the world of open-source intelligence.

Chapter 8: Data Analysis and Visualization for OSINT Professionals

Mastering data analysis techniques is a journey that opens doors to valuable insights and informed decision-making in various domains and professions.

Data analysis is a process of inspecting, cleaning, transforming, and interpreting data with the goal of discovering useful information, drawing conclusions, and supporting decision-making.

It involves a wide range of methods, tools, and approaches that enable you to extract knowledge from data.

One fundamental aspect of mastering data analysis is acquiring a deep understanding of the data itself.

Before you can analyze data, you must become intimately familiar with its sources, characteristics, and quality.

This step often involves data collection, which can include gathering data from surveys, experiments, databases, or even public sources like the internet.

Once you have the data in hand, the next step is data preprocessing.

Data preprocessing involves cleaning and transforming the raw data into a format suitable for analysis.

This can include dealing with missing values, handling outliers, and ensuring data consistency.

Data preprocessing is a critical phase because the quality of your analysis depends on the quality of the data you work with.

Exploratory data analysis (EDA) is an essential technique in data analysis.

EDA involves visualizing and summarizing data to gain insights, detect patterns, and generate hypotheses.

Graphs, charts, and summary statistics are common tools used in EDA to understand data distribution, relationships between variables, and potential outliers.

Understanding the data's distribution helps you choose appropriate statistical methods for analysis.

Inferential statistics are often used to draw conclusions about a population based on a sample.

Hypothesis testing, confidence intervals, and regression analysis are examples of inferential statistical techniques.

These methods allow you to make inferences about the population parameters from which your data was drawn.

Mastering inferential statistics requires a deep understanding of probability theory and statistical models.

Descriptive statistics, on the other hand, focus on summarizing and describing data.

Measures of central tendency, such as mean, median, and mode, provide information about the typical value in a dataset.

Measures of variability, like standard deviation and range, indicate how spread out the data is.

Descriptive statistics help you communicate the main characteristics of your data succinctly.

Data visualization is an indispensable tool in data analysis.

Effective data visualization allows you to convey complex information in a clear and intuitive manner.

Visualizations can be used to explore data, communicate results, and identify trends or outliers.

Common types of data visualizations include bar charts, line graphs, scatter plots, and heatmaps.

Choosing the right visualization method depends on the data's nature and the message you want to convey.

Regression analysis is a powerful technique for understanding the relationship between variables.

It allows you to model the relationship between a dependent variable and one or more independent variables.

Linear regression is a widely used method for modeling linear relationships, while nonlinear regression models more complex relationships.

Regression analysis can be applied to a wide range of fields, from economics to biology, to predict outcomes or understand underlying patterns.

Machine learning is a field of data analysis that has gained prominence in recent years.

Machine learning algorithms allow you to build predictive models and make data-driven decisions without explicitly programming rules.

Supervised learning, unsupervised learning, and reinforcement learning are common categories of machine learning techniques.

Supervised learning involves training a model on labeled data to predict outcomes, while unsupervised learning seeks to discover patterns or groupings within unlabeled data.

Reinforcement learning focuses on decision-making in dynamic environments.

Mastering machine learning requires a solid foundation in mathematics, programming, and a deep understanding of various algorithms.

Time series analysis is a specialized technique used for data that is collected over time.

Time series data often exhibits temporal patterns, trends, and seasonality.

Analyzing time series data involves techniques like autoregressive integrated moving average (ARIMA) modeling, exponential smoothing, and Fourier analysis.

Time series analysis is commonly used in finance, economics, and environmental science, among other fields.

Cluster analysis is a technique used to group similar data points together.

It is a form of unsupervised learning and can be applied to tasks such as customer segmentation, image recognition, and anomaly detection.

Common clustering algorithms include k-means, hierarchical clustering, and DBSCAN.

Choosing the right clustering algorithm depends on the data and the problem you are trying to solve.

Dimensionality reduction techniques are essential when dealing with high-dimensional data.

These techniques aim to reduce the number of variables while preserving the essential information.

Principal component analysis (PCA) and t-distributed stochastic neighbor embedding (t-SNE) are examples of dimensionality reduction methods.

They help simplify data visualization and analysis by transforming data into a lower-dimensional space.

Text analysis, also known as text mining or natural language processing (NLP), deals with the extraction of insights from textual data.

Text analysis techniques include text classification, sentiment analysis, topic modeling, and named entity recognition.

Text analysis is invaluable in fields like marketing, social media analysis, and content recommendation.

Spatial analysis focuses on data that has a geographic component.

Geographic information systems (GIS) are widely used tools for spatial analysis.

Spatial analysis can be applied to tasks such as mapping, geostatistics, and spatial modeling.

It is essential in fields like urban planning, epidemiology, and environmental science.

Advanced data analysis often involves programming and scripting.

Languages like Python and R are popular choices for data analysis due to their extensive libraries and data manipulation capabilities.

Mastering programming for data analysis allows you to automate repetitive tasks, create custom solutions, and work efficiently with large datasets.

Ethical considerations are critical in data analysis.

Data privacy, consent, and responsible data handling are paramount.

It's essential to adhere to ethical guidelines and regulations, especially when dealing with sensitive or personal data.

Mastering data analysis techniques requires continuous learning and practice.

The field of data analysis is dynamic, with new tools and methodologies constantly emerging.

Staying up to date with the latest developments and best practices is essential for success in this field.

In summary, mastering data analysis techniques is a multidimensional journey that encompasses various skills, from data collection and preprocessing to statistical analysis, machine learning, and specialized techniques like time series analysis, cluster analysis, and text analysis.

Ethical considerations and programming proficiency are also vital components of data analysis expertise.

With a solid foundation and ongoing learning, you can become a proficient data analyst capable of extracting valuable insights from data in various domains and applications.

Visualizing OSINT data is a crucial step in the open-source intelligence (OSINT) process, as it transforms raw information into actionable insights.

Data visualization is a powerful technique that helps analysts and investigators make sense of vast amounts of data by presenting it in a visually digestible format.

Effective data visualization not only conveys complex information but also aids in detecting patterns, trends, and anomalies that might otherwise remain hidden.

By visualizing OSINT data, you can enhance your understanding of the information at hand and draw valuable conclusions.

One fundamental principle of data visualization is choosing the right type of visualization for your data.

Different types of data require different types of visual representations.

For example, bar charts are suitable for comparing categories, line graphs for showing trends over time, and scatter plots for identifying correlations.

Choosing the appropriate visualization method depends on the nature of your OSINT data and the specific insights you aim to extract.

Consider the story you want to tell with your data and select the visualization that best serves that narrative.

Bar charts are a common choice for OSINT data visualization when you need to compare discrete categories.

They use vertical or horizontal bars to represent the values of different categories, making it easy to spot differences and similarities.

In OSINT, bar charts can be employed to compare the number of mentions of specific keywords across different sources or to analyze the distribution of social media posts by location.

Line graphs are suitable for showing trends and changes over time.

They use lines to connect data points, allowing you to observe how a variable evolves over a specific period.

In OSINT, line graphs can be useful for tracking the frequency of certain events or keywords in online discussions over time.

For instance, you might use a line graph to visualize the fluctuation of public sentiment regarding a particular topic.

Scatter plots are valuable when you want to explore the relationship between two variables.

They display individual data points on a two-dimensional grid, with each point representing a combination of values from the two variables.

In OSINT, scatter plots can help identify correlations between factors, such as the relationship between the frequency of online mentions of a product and its sales figures.

Heatmaps are a powerful tool for visualizing large datasets, especially when dealing with geographical or spatial data.

They use color gradients to represent the density of data points in different regions.

In OSINT, heatmaps can be employed to visualize the concentration of social media posts, incidents, or mentions on a map, revealing hotspots or patterns.

Network graphs are essential for understanding relationships and connections within data.

They represent entities as nodes and relationships as edges, providing a visual representation of the network structure.

In OSINT, network graphs can be used to visualize social networks, connections between individuals, or the flow of information between different online communities.

Word clouds are a creative way to visualize text data.

They display words from a dataset in varying sizes, with the size of each word indicating its frequency.

Word clouds are often used in OSINT to quickly identify keywords, topics, or trends in online discussions or documents.

Geospatial maps are vital for OSINT investigations that involve location data.

They allow you to visualize information on a map, providing insights into the geographical distribution of events, incidents, or mentions.

Geospatial maps can be used to track the movement of individuals, the locations of social media posts, or the distribution of specific incidents.

Interactive dashboards offer a dynamic and user-friendly way to explore and analyze OSINT data.

They combine various types of visualizations and filters, enabling users to interact with the data and customize their views.

Interactive dashboards are particularly useful for OSINT professionals who need to explore data in real-time or collaborate with others.

Choosing the appropriate visualization tool is just as important as selecting the right visualization type.

There are various software tools available for creating data visualizations, each with its strengths and capabilities.

Common tools for OSINT data visualization include Tableau, Power BI, Google Data Studio, and Python libraries like Matplotlib and Plotly.

The choice of tool depends on factors such as your data source, your familiarity with the tool, and the specific requirements of your OSINT project.

Once you have selected the appropriate visualization tool and type, the next step is to prepare your data for visualization.

This involves cleaning and formatting the data to ensure it is in a suitable structure for creating visualizations.

Data cleaning may involve removing duplicates, handling missing values, and converting data types as needed.

Formatting data for visualization is crucial to ensure that the visualization tool can interpret and display the information correctly.

When designing OSINT visualizations, consider the principles of effective data communication.

Your visualizations should have clear titles, labels, and legends to provide context and guidance to the audience.

Avoid clutter and unnecessary elements that can distract from the main message.

Use color strategically to highlight important information and ensure that your visualizations are accessible to all users, including those with color blindness.

Interactivity can enhance the utility of OSINT visualizations.

Interactive features like tooltips, filters, and zoom options allow users to explore the data in more detail.

By enabling interactivity, you empower your audience to investigate the data on their terms and gain deeper insights.

Sharing OSINT visualizations is an essential aspect of the analysis process.

You should be able to present your findings to stakeholders, colleagues, or clients effectively.

Most visualization tools offer options for exporting visualizations as images, interactive web pages, or even embedding them in reports or presentations.

Consider the best format for sharing your OSINT visualizations based on your audience's needs and preferences.

Finally, keep in mind that data visualization is not just about creating pretty pictures; it's about extracting actionable insights from data.

As an OSINT practitioner, your goal is to uncover meaningful patterns, trends, or anomalies that can inform decisions, identify risks, or support investigations.

Effective data visualization is a valuable skill that enhances your ability to achieve these objectives in the world of open-source intelligence.

In summary, visualizing OSINT data is a critical step in the OSINT process that transforms raw information into actionable insights.

By choosing the right visualization type, employing the appropriate visualization tool, and following best practices in data preparation and design, you can create compelling and informative visualizations that enhance your understanding of the data and aid in decision-making.

Chapter 9: Ethical Considerations and Legal Implications

Ethical guidelines are paramount in the practice of open-source intelligence (OSINT) to ensure that investigations and information gathering are conducted responsibly and within legal and moral boundaries.

OSINT practitioners play a significant role in collecting and analyzing publicly available information from various sources, including the internet, social media, and public records.

These professionals often deal with sensitive and personal data, making ethical considerations crucial in their work.

One fundamental ethical principle in OSINT is respect for privacy.

OSINT practitioners must be diligent in protecting the privacy rights of individuals whose information may be collected during investigations.

This includes refraining from intrusive or unethical data collection methods and ensuring that information is used solely for legitimate purposes.

Informed consent is another key ethical principle in OSINT.

Before collecting or using information from publicly available sources, it is essential to consider whether the individuals involved have given their explicit consent for the data to be used in the manner intended.

While much of the data in OSINT is publicly accessible, practitioners must still respect the boundaries set by the individuals or entities being investigated.

Transparency is a vital component of ethical OSINT practices.

Practitioners should strive to be transparent about their objectives and the methods they employ when conducting investigations.

This transparency helps build trust and credibility with both the public and any relevant stakeholders.

When engaging in OSINT activities, it is essential to be honest and truthful in the representation of findings.

Falsifying or misrepresenting information undermines the integrity of the entire process and can have legal consequences.

OSINT practitioners should also adhere to the principle of accuracy, ensuring that the information they collect and disseminate is as precise as possible.

Inaccurate or misleading information can have severe consequences and damage the credibility of the practitioner and the organizations they represent.

Objectivity is a critical ethical guideline in OSINT.

Practitioners should strive to remain impartial and avoid biases or preconceived notions that could influence their investigations.

The goal is to provide unbiased and objective assessments based on the available data.

Responsible information handling is essential in OSINT.

Practitioners should exercise care in storing, sharing, and disposing of collected data to prevent unauthorized access or misuse.

This includes protecting sensitive information and ensuring data security.

The principle of proportionality dictates that OSINT practitioners should only collect and use information that is directly relevant to their investigative objectives.

Collecting excessive or irrelevant data can infringe on privacy rights and ethical standards.

Respect for the law is a fundamental ethical guideline.

Practitioners must comply with all applicable laws and regulations while conducting OSINT activities.

This includes respecting copyright, intellectual property, and data protection laws.

In many cases, OSINT practitioners are required to obtain legal permissions or approvals before conducting certain types of investigations.

Additionally, OSINT practitioners should be aware of the international legal framework and any restrictions on data collection and sharing across borders.

Confidentiality is crucial in OSINT, particularly in cases where sensitive or classified information is involved.

Practitioners should maintain the confidentiality of their work and the information they handle, sharing it only with authorized individuals or entities.

In cases where OSINT practitioners work as part of a team or organization, they should adhere to internal policies and procedures related to information security and confidentiality.

Ethical OSINT practitioners should always be aware of the potential consequences of their work.

Information collected during investigations can have real-world impacts on individuals, organizations, or even nations.

Practitioners should consider the potential harm that may result from their actions and take steps to mitigate any adverse effects.

Ethical OSINT practices also extend to the responsible reporting of findings.

Practitioners should ensure that their reports are clear, accurate, and actionable, providing valuable insights without sensationalism or distortion.

Reporting should be done in a manner that respects the privacy and dignity of individuals involved.

In the age of digital and online investigations, ethical OSINT practices also include cybersecurity measures.

Practitioners should protect their own digital identities and data to prevent unauthorized access or malicious attacks that could compromise their work.

This includes safeguarding sensitive information and using secure communication channels.

In summary, ethical guidelines in OSINT are essential to ensure that investigations and information gathering are conducted responsibly, transparently, and within legal and moral boundaries.

OSINT practitioners must adhere to principles such as privacy, informed consent, transparency, honesty, accuracy, objectivity, responsible information handling, proportionality, respect for the law, confidentiality, awareness of consequences, responsible reporting, and cybersecurity.

By following these ethical guidelines, OSINT practitioners can maintain the integrity of their work and contribute to the responsible use of open-source intelligence in various fields and contexts.

Legal challenges and compliance are integral aspects of any open-source intelligence (OSINT) operation, as practitioners must navigate a complex landscape of laws and regulations to ensure that their activities remain lawful and ethically sound.

OSINT, by its nature, involves the collection and analysis of information from publicly available sources, but it must be done within the confines of legal frameworks to protect the rights and privacy of individuals and organizations.

One of the primary legal challenges in OSINT is the tension between the right to privacy and the right to information.

Balancing these rights can be intricate, as OSINT practitioners must respect individuals' privacy while accessing information that is, by definition, publicly available.

Understanding and complying with data protection laws, such as the European Union's General Data Protection Regulation (GDPR), is essential, as they regulate the processing of personal data.

In some jurisdictions, the collection of certain types of information or the use of specific OSINT techniques may require informed consent or legal authorization.

Navigating these legal requirements can be complex and depends on the specific jurisdiction and the nature of the information being collected.

Intellectual property rights are another crucial aspect of legal compliance in OSINT.

Practitioners must be aware of copyright laws and ensure they do not infringe on intellectual property rights when collecting or sharing information.

This includes respecting copyright protections for documents, images, and other media found online.

It is essential to attribute sources properly and refrain from unauthorized use.

Additionally, OSINT practitioners must consider the legality of web scraping and data harvesting activities, as they can potentially infringe on terms of service agreements or violate anti-bot policies on websites.

In some cases, web scraping may be explicitly prohibited, and practitioners should respect these restrictions.

Ensuring that OSINT activities comply with applicable privacy laws is of utmost importance.

Practitioners should be aware of the legal frameworks that govern the collection, processing, and storage of personal information, both within their own jurisdiction and in the jurisdictions where they operate.

This includes understanding the definition of personal data, the conditions for lawful processing, and the rights of data subjects.

When collecting OSINT data that may contain personal information, it is crucial to adhere to privacy regulations and obtain any necessary permissions or consents.

Additionally, OSINT practitioners should implement data protection measures to safeguard the personal information they handle.

Compliance with international data protection standards, such as GDPR, is essential when dealing with data from European individuals or entities.

Respecting ethical considerations and the principles of responsible OSINT is a vital component of legal compliance.

Ethical OSINT practices often align with legal requirements, as adhering to ethical guidelines can help ensure that practitioners do not engage in activities that could be considered unlawful or unethical.

Practitioners should exercise transparency, honesty, and accuracy in their OSINT activities, providing clear and truthful representations of their findings.

Ensuring that OSINT activities do not cross into areas that could be construed as harassment, cyberbullying, or cyberstalking is essential for legal compliance.

Furthermore, respecting the principle of proportionality is vital, ensuring that OSINT practitioners collect and use only the information necessary for their legitimate investigative purposes.

Responsible reporting of findings is also a legal and ethical imperative.

Practitioners should be cautious when disseminating information and avoid making unfounded accusations or assumptions that could harm an individual's reputation or violate their rights.

When sharing OSINT findings, it is essential to follow the principle of accuracy and substantiate claims with credible evidence.

In cases where OSINT practitioners work as part of a team or an organization, they should adhere to internal policies and procedures related to legal compliance and ethical conduct.

These policies may include guidelines for data protection, information sharing, and responsible reporting.

International OSINT activities present unique legal challenges related to jurisdiction and cross-border data sharing.

Practitioners operating in different countries or dealing with information from diverse sources must be mindful of the legal requirements in each jurisdiction.

International legal frameworks, such as mutual legal assistance treaties (MLATs), can facilitate cross-border cooperation in OSINT investigations.

However, navigating the complexities of international law and agreements requires careful consideration and legal expertise.

The use of OSINT tools and techniques can also present legal challenges.

Some tools may be subject to export controls or fall under specific regulations due to their capabilities or intended use.

Practitioners should be aware of any legal restrictions that may apply to the acquisition or use of OSINT tools and technologies.

Additionally, practitioners should consider the legality of automated OSINT techniques, such as web scraping or data mining, and ensure they comply with relevant laws and regulations.

Ethical hacking and penetration testing, which often involve OSINT, must be conducted in compliance with applicable cybersecurity and computer crime laws.

Practitioners should obtain proper authorization and permissions before engaging in such activities to avoid legal repercussions.

When conducting OSINT investigations that involve social media or online communities, practitioners should be cautious not to engage in deceptive practices or manipulation.

Creating fake profiles, spreading disinformation, or engaging in harmful online behavior can lead to legal consequences and ethical dilemmas.

In summary, legal challenges and compliance are essential considerations in the practice of open-source intelligence.

OSINT practitioners must navigate a complex legal landscape, respecting privacy rights, intellectual property, data protection laws, and international regulations.

Adhering to ethical guidelines and responsible OSINT practices not only helps ensure legal compliance but also upholds the integrity and credibility of OSINT investigations.

Chapter 10: OSINT Case Studies and Real-World Scenarios

OSINT success stories exemplify the remarkable impact of open-source intelligence in a wide range of fields, showcasing its potential to uncover critical information, solve complex problems, and shape decision-making processes.

These stories illuminate the valuable insights that OSINT can provide, often with real-world consequences.

One compelling OSINT success story involves the identification of criminal activities through social media analysis.

In a particular case, law enforcement agencies used OSINT techniques to monitor and analyze social media posts related to illegal drug trafficking.

By examining publicly available posts and comments, investigators were able to identify individuals involved in the drug trade, their networks, and even specific locations where drug transactions were likely to occur.

This information proved instrumental in launching successful operations and apprehending suspects.

Another noteworthy OSINT success story relates to humanitarian efforts during natural disasters.

In the aftermath of a devastating earthquake, OSINT practitioners collaborated with disaster relief organizations to analyze social media data, satellite imagery, and online forums.

By leveraging these open-source resources, they quickly identified areas with the most significant damage, assessed the needs of affected communities, and mobilized resources effectively.

This expedited response helped save lives and provided critical support to those in distress.

In the realm of corporate security, OSINT has played a crucial role in identifying vulnerabilities and threats to businesses.

In one instance, a multinational corporation sought to assess its online exposure and susceptibility to cyberattacks.

OSINT specialists conducted a comprehensive analysis of the company's digital footprint, identifying potential weak points, exposed credentials, and information leaks.

This proactive approach allowed the company to strengthen its cybersecurity measures and mitigate potential risks before they could be exploited by malicious actors.

OSINT has also demonstrated its effectiveness in geopolitical analysis and international relations.

In a notable case, OSINT analysts closely monitored online discussions and news reports surrounding a diplomatic conflict between two countries.

By collecting and analyzing open-source information, they were able to discern shifts in rhetoric, predict potential escalations, and advise policymakers on diplomatic strategies.

Their timely insights contributed to de-escalating tensions and facilitating diplomatic negotiations.

Furthermore, OSINT has been instrumental in countering disinformation campaigns and ensuring the integrity of democratic processes.

During a national election, OSINT experts collaborated with government agencies to identify and analyze false narratives, fake news, and foreign interference efforts.

By tracking the dissemination of misleading information on social media platforms and open online forums, they were able to inform the public and enhance cybersecurity measures to protect the electoral process.

OSINT has also proved invaluable in uncovering human rights abuses and advocating for justice.

In a harrowing case, OSINT practitioners collected and verified open-source evidence, including photos, videos, and witness testimonies, to document a genocide occurring in a conflict-ridden region.

Their efforts brought international attention to the crisis, prompted humanitarian aid, and led to calls for accountability at the highest levels of government.

The field of OSINT has witnessed remarkable advancements, such as the use of artificial intelligence and machine learning algorithms to process vast amounts of open-source data.

In a cutting-edge OSINT success story, researchers developed AI-driven tools that could analyze satellite imagery to detect illegal deforestation in remote areas.

These tools identified areas of environmental concern, enabling conservation organizations and governments to take targeted actions against illegal logging operations.

Moreover, OSINT has been a game-changer in the realm of law enforcement and counterterrorism efforts.

In a critical operation, intelligence agencies leveraged OSINT techniques to track the online activities of a terrorist organization.

Through the analysis of publicly available information, they identified recruitment networks, communication channels, and key operatives.

This OSINT-driven intelligence facilitated the disruption of terrorist plots and the apprehension of individuals involved in extremist activities.

In the context of financial investigations and fraud prevention, OSINT has provided critical leads and evidence.

In a complex case of corporate fraud, forensic accountants and OSINT experts collaborated to trace hidden assets, uncover financial irregularities, and expose fraudulent transactions.

Their comprehensive analysis of open-source financial data contributed to successful litigation and financial recovery.

These OSINT success stories underscore the versatile and powerful nature of open-source intelligence.

Whether applied to law enforcement, humanitarian efforts, cybersecurity, diplomacy, human rights advocacy, environmental conservation, or counterterrorism, OSINT continues to demonstrate its capacity to make a positive impact on society.

As technology and methodologies evolve, OSINT remains a vital tool for uncovering hidden truths, informing decision-makers, and promoting transparency in an increasingly interconnected world.

Practical OSINT scenarios and solutions provide valuable insights into how open-source intelligence can be applied in real-world situations to address specific challenges and achieve desired outcomes.

These scenarios illustrate the versatility of OSINT techniques and the critical role they play in various domains.

Consider a scenario involving a cybersecurity breach within a company's network.

In this situation, an OSINT practitioner can employ a combination of techniques to investigate the breach, identify the source of the attack, and assess the extent of the compromise.

One solution involves analyzing the attacker's digital footprint by examining social media profiles, forum posts, and publicly available online discussions related to hacking techniques and tools.

By correlating this information with the timing of the breach, the practitioner can gain valuable insights into potential threat actors and their motivations.

Additionally, OSINT can be used to search for leaked credentials or compromised data on the dark web or underground forums, helping the organization understand the scope of the breach and take appropriate remediation measures.

Another practical OSINT scenario revolves around due diligence in business transactions.

Imagine a company considering a merger or acquisition with another organization.

To ensure a comprehensive evaluation, OSINT practitioners can conduct in-depth research on the target company and its key stakeholders.

This involves examining publicly available financial records, news articles, social media profiles, and legal filings to assess the financial health, reputation, and potential risks associated with the target.

By scrutinizing the digital presence of executives and board members, OSINT can uncover any red flags, such as previous legal issues or controversies, which may impact the decision-making process.

Furthermore, OSINT can aid in identifying any undisclosed affiliations or conflicts of interest that could affect the outcome of the transaction.

In the realm of competitive intelligence, a practical OSINT scenario may involve a company seeking to gain an edge in its industry.

OSINT can be employed to gather information on competitors, market trends, and emerging technologies.

One solution involves monitoring social media channels, industry forums, and news sources to track competitors' product launches, partnerships, and strategic initiatives.

This information can inform the company's own product development and marketing strategies.

Moreover, OSINT can be used to identify potential vulnerabilities or weaknesses in competitors' online presence, such as unsecured databases or exposed sensitive information.

By proactively addressing these issues, the company can enhance its competitive position.

A practical OSINT scenario in the field of law enforcement and public safety centers around tracking and apprehending a fugitive.

In this situation, OSINT practitioners can leverage publicly available information to locate the individual and gather intelligence on their activities.

One solution involves analyzing the fugitive's social media posts, online interactions, and geotagged photos to establish a pattern of behavior and potential hiding places.

By cross-referencing this digital footprint with public records, travel histories, and known associates, law enforcement can narrow down the search area and allocate resources effectively.

Furthermore, OSINT can be used to monitor online marketplaces, cryptocurrency transactions, and communication channels that the fugitive may use to sustain themselves while on the run.

This comprehensive OSINT approach increases the likelihood of a successful apprehension.

Another practical OSINT scenario pertains to geopolitical analysis and crisis response.

Consider a situation involving a diplomatic crisis between two nations.

OSINT can play a critical role in monitoring the development of the crisis, understanding the motivations of the involved parties, and providing timely insights to decision-makers.

One solution involves monitoring international news sources, government statements, and official social media accounts to track changes in rhetoric, policy shifts, and diplomatic maneuvers.

By analyzing open-source information, OSINT practitioners can identify potential triggers for escalation and advise on diplomatic strategies to de-escalate tensions.

Additionally, OSINT can be used to monitor social media sentiment and public reactions, providing valuable feedback on the effectiveness of crisis communication efforts.

A practical OSINT scenario in the realm of humanitarian aid and disaster response revolves around assessing the impact of a natural disaster in a remote area.

In such situations, OSINT can help humanitarian organizations rapidly gather information to guide their response efforts.

One solution involves analyzing satellite imagery, social media posts, and crowd-sourced data to assess the extent of damage, identify areas in need of assistance, and estimate the number of affected individuals.

By harnessing OSINT, organizations can prioritize resource allocation, plan logistics, and coordinate relief efforts more effectively.

Furthermore, OSINT can be used to identify local resources, such as medical facilities and volunteer networks, that can be mobilized to provide immediate assistance.
Practical OSINT scenarios and solutions continue to evolve as technology and information sources expand.

These scenarios demonstrate the relevance and applicability of OSINT across diverse fields, from cybersecurity and business intelligence to law enforcement, diplomacy, and humanitarian aid.

By adapting OSINT techniques to specific challenges and leveraging publicly available information, practitioners can make informed decisions, mitigate risks, and contribute to positive outcomes in a rapidly changing world.

BOOK 2
FROM NOVICE TO NINJA
MASTERING OSINT COMMANDO WITH SPOKEO,
SPIDERFOOT, SEON, AND LAMPYRE

ROB BOTWRIGHT

Chapter 1: Embracing the OSINT Journey

The evolution of open-source intelligence (OSINT) reflects a dynamic journey characterized by technological advancements, changing information landscapes, and evolving methodologies.

OSINT, as a discipline, has a rich history rooted in the practice of collecting and analyzing publicly available information to support decision-making processes.

In the early days of OSINT, practitioners relied primarily on traditional sources of information, such as newspapers, magazines, books, and government publications.

The collection and dissemination of data were often labor-intensive and time-consuming, requiring manual research and data extraction.

The advent of the internet in the late 20th century marked a significant turning point in the evolution of OSINT.

The digital revolution brought about unprecedented access to vast amounts of online information, transforming the way OSINT practitioners operated.

The proliferation of websites, online forums, social media platforms, and digital archives expanded the sources of open-source information exponentially.

This shift enabled OSINT practitioners to harness the power of technology to access and analyze information more efficiently.

The emergence of search engines, web scraping tools, and data aggregation platforms revolutionized the collection phase of OSINT.

Practitioners could now conduct targeted keyword searches, automate data retrieval, and consolidate information from multiple online sources.

This automation greatly accelerated the pace of OSINT investigations and made it possible to monitor developments in real-time.

Additionally, the integration of geospatial data and mapping technologies allowed OSINT practitioners to visualize and analyze location-based information, enhancing their ability to understand complex scenarios.

The evolution of social media platforms played a pivotal role in reshaping the OSINT landscape.

Social media platforms became rich sources of real-time information, offering insights into public sentiment, events, and trends.

OSINT practitioners adapted their methodologies to include the monitoring of social media channels, where they could track breaking news, public reactions, and emerging narratives.

These platforms also facilitated the analysis of user-generated content, including photos, videos, and user-generated geotags, providing valuable context for OSINT investigations.

However, the surge in online disinformation and the spread of fake news presented new challenges for OSINT practitioners.

Distinguishing between credible information and false or manipulated content became a critical aspect of OSINT analysis.

To address this challenge, practitioners developed techniques to verify the authenticity of digital content and assess the credibility of sources.

The use of digital forensics, image analysis, and metadata examination became essential tools in the OSINT toolkit.

Machine learning and artificial intelligence (AI) have further advanced the field of OSINT.

These technologies enable automated content analysis, sentiment analysis, and the identification of patterns and anomalies within large datasets.

OSINT practitioners can leverage AI-driven tools to process and categorize vast amounts of open-source information, uncover hidden insights, and detect emerging trends.

Machine learning algorithms can assist in identifying potential threats, monitoring online communities, and predicting future events based on historical data.

Moreover, OSINT practitioners have embraced collaborative platforms and online communities to share knowledge, best practices, and emerging techniques.

These forums provide a space for experts and enthusiasts to exchange ideas, tools, and methodologies, fostering innovation and continuous improvement in the field.

As the digital landscape continues to evolve, OSINT practitioners must adapt to emerging challenges and opportunities.

The proliferation of encrypted communication channels and the use of virtual private networks (VPNs) by threat actors have made some aspects of OSINT collection more challenging.

Practitioners need to explore innovative approaches to access information while respecting privacy and legal boundaries.

Additionally, the ethical considerations surrounding OSINT have gained prominence.

Practitioners must navigate a complex landscape of privacy rights, consent, and responsible information handling.

Ensuring that OSINT activities align with ethical guidelines and legal requirements is paramount to maintaining the integrity of the field.

The future of OSINT promises continued evolution as technology advances.

Advancements in data analytics, natural language processing, and machine learning will empower OSINT practitioners to extract even deeper insights from open-source information.

Real-time monitoring of social media sentiment and emerging narratives will become more sophisticated, enabling quicker response to crises and events.

Geospatial analysis will continue to play a crucial role in understanding location-based information, especially in the context of disaster response, humanitarian aid, and environmental monitoring.

Collaborative efforts between governments, academia, and the private sector will drive innovation and the development of cutting-edge OSINT tools and methodologies.

The integration of OSINT into broader intelligence and decision-making processes will become increasingly seamless, providing decision-makers with timely and relevant insights to inform strategic choices.

In summary, the evolution of open-source intelligence is a testament to its adaptability and relevance in an information-driven world.

From its origins in traditional research to the digital age of automation and artificial intelligence, OSINT has continually transformed to meet the demands of an ever-changing landscape.

As OSINT practitioners continue to harness the power of technology, collaboration, and ethical principles, the field will undoubtedly play an increasingly vital role in supporting a wide range of endeavors, from cybersecurity and national security to humanitarian aid and business intelligence.

Your role in the OSINT landscape is multifaceted and can have a significant impact on various domains and industries.

As an OSINT practitioner, you contribute to the collection, analysis, and dissemination of open-source information, providing valuable insights that inform decisions and actions. Your first responsibility in the OSINT landscape is to understand the ethical considerations that underpin the discipline.

You must adhere to principles of transparency, accuracy, and responsibility in your information gathering and reporting.

Respecting privacy rights, consent, and legal boundaries is essential to maintain the integrity of OSINT activities.

Your role as an OSINT practitioner involves staying up-to-date with the latest tools, techniques, and technologies.

Continual learning and professional development are crucial to ensure that you can effectively navigate the evolving information landscape.

You should be proficient in the use of OSINT tools such as search engines, web scraping applications, and social media monitoring platforms.

Additionally, familiarity with data analysis and visualization tools will enhance your ability to extract meaningful insights from open-source information.

Collaboration is a fundamental aspect of your role in the OSINT landscape.

You may work as part of a team, sharing expertise and insights with colleagues to tackle complex challenges.

Collaborative platforms and online communities provide spaces for knowledge exchange and innovation within the OSINT community.

In your role, you must maintain a critical mindset and exercise discernment in your information analysis.

Not all open-source information is reliable or accurate, and distinguishing between credible sources and false or manipulated content is essential.

You should be proficient in digital forensics and image analysis to verify the authenticity of digital content.

Your role in the OSINT landscape extends to addressing the challenges posed by disinformation and fake news.

Developing techniques to detect and counter false narratives is crucial to maintaining the credibility of OSINT analysis.

When conducting OSINT investigations, your role includes understanding the legal frameworks that govern data collection and information sharing.

Compliance with data protection laws and regulations, both within your jurisdiction and internationally, is essential to avoid legal repercussions.

Your role as an OSINT practitioner may involve conducting investigations for various purposes.

These purposes could range from cybersecurity and corporate due diligence to humanitarian aid and law enforcement.

Adapting your methodologies and approaches to meet the specific objectives of each investigation is part of your responsibility.

Your role also includes contributing to the protection of privacy rights and the responsible use of open-source information.

Ensuring that your OSINT activities do not infringe on individuals' privacy or engage in unethical practices is essential.

Additionally, your role may require you to educate and raise awareness about OSINT best practices and ethical guidelines.

Sharing your knowledge with others in your organization or community can help promote responsible and effective OSINT practices.

In some cases, your role may involve working with decision-makers, providing them with actionable insights based on your OSINT findings.

Communicating complex information in a clear and understandable manner is an important aspect of this responsibility.

Your role in the OSINT landscape extends to anticipating and adapting to emerging challenges and opportunities.

As technology evolves and new information sources emerge, you should be prepared to explore innovative approaches and tools.

Collaboration with experts from various fields, such as cybersecurity, data science, and international relations, can enhance your capabilities as an OSINT practitioner.

Your role includes being adaptable and flexible in your approaches to information gathering and analysis.

Different investigations may require different strategies, and your ability to tailor your methods to each situation is a valuable asset.

Overall, your role in the OSINT landscape is one of responsibility, ethics, continuous learning, collaboration, and adaptability.

By fulfilling these responsibilities effectively, you contribute to the positive impact of OSINT across various domains and industries, helping organizations and decision-makers make informed choices based on reliable and actionable information.

Chapter 2: Building a Solid Foundation in OSINT

OSINT fundamentals encompass the core principles and concepts that underpin the discipline of open-source intelligence.

As an OSINT practitioner, understanding these fundamentals is essential to navigate the information landscape effectively and conduct meaningful investigations.

One of the key OSINT fundamentals is the concept of open sources.

Open sources refer to publicly available information that can be accessed without breaching legal or ethical boundaries.

These sources include newspapers, websites, social media platforms, public records, government publications, and more.

The accessibility of open sources distinguishes OSINT from other forms of intelligence gathering.

Another fundamental concept in OSINT is the principle of transparency.

Transparency means that OSINT practitioners openly and honestly disclose their identity and purpose when interacting with online sources or individuals.

Maintaining transparency is essential to adhere to ethical guidelines and establish trust within the online community.

Additionally, OSINT practitioners should respect the privacy and consent of individuals and organizations whose information they access.

Ethical considerations are at the core of OSINT fundamentals.

Ethical OSINT practices involve conducting investigations in a responsible, lawful, and respectful manner.

OSINT practitioners should avoid engaging in deceptive practices, harassment, or any activities that violate privacy or legal boundaries.

Accuracy and reliability are paramount in OSINT.

Information gathered through open sources must be carefully verified and cross-referenced to ensure its accuracy.

Relying on unverified information can lead to erroneous conclusions and potentially harmful consequences.

One of the fundamental OSINT techniques is information collection.

Information collection involves systematically gathering data from a wide range of open sources.

This process may include searching online databases, scraping websites, monitoring social media, and accessing public records.

OSINT practitioners use various tools and methods to collect information efficiently and comprehensively.

Analysis is another critical aspect of OSINT fundamentals.

Once information is collected, it must be analyzed to extract meaningful insights.

Analysis involves identifying patterns, connections, and trends within the data to generate actionable intelligence.

Effective analysis requires critical thinking and the ability to draw informed conclusions from open-source information.

The dissemination of OSINT findings is another fundamental component.

OSINT practitioners should communicate their findings clearly and responsibly to relevant stakeholders, whether they are decision-makers, organizations, or the public.

Timely and accurate reporting is essential to support informed decision-making.

The OSINT landscape is rich with terminology and jargon that practitioners must understand.

One common term in OSINT is "doxing," which refers to the act of researching and revealing private or personal information about an individual or organization without their consent.

Doxing is generally considered unethical and can have legal repercussions.

"Geolocation" is another important term in OSINT.

Geolocation involves determining the physical location of an individual or object based on available data, such as IP addresses, GPS coordinates, or geotagged photos.

Geolocation can be a valuable tool for OSINT investigations.

"Metadata" is a term that OSINT practitioners encounter frequently.

Metadata refers to the information embedded in digital files, such as photos, documents, or videos.

This information can include details about the file's creation, authorship, and modification history, which can be useful in OSINT analysis.

"Deep web" and "dark web" are terms often used in OSINT.

The deep web refers to parts of the internet not indexed by traditional search engines, such as password-protected databases or subscription-based content.

The dark web, on the other hand, is a part of the deep web that is intentionally hidden and often associated with illegal activities.

Understanding the distinction between these terms is crucial for OSINT practitioners.

"Scraping" is a term used to describe the automated process of extracting data from websites.

Web scraping tools allow OSINT practitioners to collect information from multiple web pages efficiently.

"Social engineering" is a term that refers to the manipulation of individuals or organizations to reveal confidential information or perform actions that may compromise security.

Social engineering techniques can be used to exploit human vulnerabilities in OSINT investigations.

"OSINT footprint" or "digital footprint" refers to the traces individuals or organizations leave online through their activities, such as social media posts, online profiles, and digital interactions.

OSINT practitioners often analyze digital footprints to gather information about their subjects.

The term "sockpuppet" is used to describe a fake or deceptive online identity created to engage in online activities anonymously or manipulate information.

Identifying sockpuppets is essential in OSINT investigations to uncover potential disinformation campaigns or malicious actors.

"False flag" operations involve creating a deceptive appearance or identity to mislead others.

In the context of OSINT, false flag operations can be used to attribute actions or information to a different source or organization.

These are just a few examples of the terminology and concepts that form the foundation of OSINT fundamentals.

Understanding and applying these fundamentals is essential for OSINT practitioners to conduct ethical, accurate, and effective investigations in the ever-evolving information landscape.

Research methodologies for OSINT are the systematic approaches and techniques used to collect, analyze, and interpret open-source information effectively.

These methodologies provide a structured framework for conducting OSINT investigations across various domains and objectives.

One of the fundamental research methodologies in OSINT is the identification of research objectives and goals.

Before beginning an OSINT investigation, it is crucial to define the specific objectives, questions, or problems that the research aims to address.

Clear research objectives help focus the investigation and guide the selection of appropriate data sources and collection methods.

Once research objectives are established, OSINT practitioners employ information collection methods.

These methods involve systematically gathering data from open sources that are relevant to the research objectives.

Information collection can include web searches, data scraping, social media monitoring, and accessing public records.

Practitioners use a combination of manual and automated techniques to collect data efficiently and comprehensively.

Data validation and verification are integral components of OSINT research methodologies.

It is essential to ensure that the information collected from open sources is accurate, reliable, and credible.

OSINT practitioners cross-reference and verify data through multiple sources or by using digital forensics and image analysis tools when dealing with multimedia content.

Data analysis is a critical phase in OSINT research methodologies.

Once information is collected, it must be analyzed to extract meaningful insights and intelligence.

Analysis involves identifying patterns, connections, and trends within the data, as well as assessing its relevance to the research objectives.

Various data analysis techniques, such as content analysis, sentiment analysis, and geospatial analysis, can be applied based on the nature of the information.

In addition to data analysis, OSINT research methodologies emphasize the importance of geolocation techniques.

Geolocation involves determining the physical location of individuals, objects, or events based on available data, such as IP addresses, GPS coordinates, or geotagged content.

Geolocation techniques are used to map and visualize information, helping OSINT practitioners understand the spatial context of open-source data.

Another essential aspect of OSINT research methodologies is the consideration of legal and ethical guidelines.

Practitioners must conduct investigations within the boundaries of applicable laws and adhere to ethical principles.

Respecting privacy rights, obtaining consent when necessary, and avoiding deceptive practices are fundamental ethical considerations in OSINT.

In some cases, OSINT research methodologies may involve covert data collection, where practitioners do not disclose their identity or purpose when accessing information.

This practice should be carried out cautiously and in strict accordance with ethical guidelines and legal requirements.

Collaboration is a key element of OSINT research methodologies.

OSINT practitioners often work as part of a team or collaborate with experts from various fields to address complex challenges.

Collaboration enables knowledge sharing, enhances data analysis, and broadens the perspective on open-source information.

Communication is an integral component of OSINT research methodologies.

Practitioners must effectively communicate their findings and insights to relevant stakeholders, whether they are decision-makers, organizations, or the public.

Clear and concise reporting is essential to support informed decision-making.

The dissemination of OSINT findings may involve the use of visual aids, reports, presentations, or interactive dashboards to convey complex information.

Time management is a practical consideration in OSINT research methodologies.

Efficiently managing the time allocated for data collection, analysis, and reporting is crucial to meet research objectives and deadlines.

OSINT practitioners may use project management tools and techniques to plan and execute investigations effectively.

Continual learning and adaptation are inherent to OSINT research methodologies.

As technology and information sources evolve, practitioners must stay updated with the latest tools, techniques, and emerging trends.

Continual learning ensures that OSINT investigations remain effective and relevant in a dynamic information landscape.

In some cases, OSINT research methodologies may involve OSINT research tools.

These tools are software applications and platforms designed to assist practitioners in various stages of the research process, from data collection and analysis to geolocation and reporting.

OSINT research tools range from web search engines and social media monitoring platforms to specialized software for data scraping, sentiment analysis, and image forensics.

OSINT research methodologies also encompass the evaluation of risks and threats.

Practitioners should assess potential risks associated with data collection, analysis, and dissemination, especially in sensitive or high-stakes investigations.

Developing risk mitigation strategies and contingency plans is part of responsible OSINT research.

Finally, OSINT research methodologies acknowledge the importance of adaptability.

Each OSINT investigation is unique, and practitioners must be prepared to adapt their methodologies, approaches, and techniques to suit the specific objectives and challenges of each research endeavor.

Flexibility and problem-solving skills are valuable attributes in the field of OSINT.

In summary, research methodologies for OSINT provide a structured framework for conducting open-source intelligence investigations effectively and ethically.

These methodologies encompass various phases, from defining research objectives and data collection to analysis, geolocation, reporting, and risk assessment.

Practitioners must also consider legal and ethical guidelines, collaboration, time management, continual learning, and adaptability to succeed in the dynamic landscape of OSINT.

Chapter 3: Spokeo Essentials for Novices

The interface of Spokeo is the gateway to accessing a wealth of open-source information about individuals, organizations, and addresses.

Understanding how to navigate and utilize Spokeo's interface is essential for OSINT practitioners and investigators.

Spokeo is a powerful online search tool that aggregates data from various sources to provide comprehensive profiles of individuals, including their contact information, social media presence, public records, and more.

The interface of Spokeo is designed to be user-friendly and intuitive, allowing users to access valuable information quickly and efficiently.

Upon entering the Spokeo website, users are greeted with a straightforward search bar, where they can input the name, email address, phone number, or physical address of the subject they wish to investigate.

The search bar serves as the starting point for all inquiries within the Spokeo interface.

Once the user enters the relevant information into the search bar and initiates a search, Spokeo's interface begins processing the query and retrieving data from its extensive database.

The search results are presented in a clear and organized manner, with each result displayed as a separate profile or entry.

Each profile typically includes a profile picture, if available, along with the subject's name, age, gender, and location.

The interface also provides a brief summary of the individual's social media presence, such as links to their Facebook, Twitter, and LinkedIn profiles.

Additionally, Spokeo's interface offers quick links to view detailed reports, which provide a more comprehensive overview of the subject's background and information.

These reports may include contact information, family members, education history, employment records, criminal records, and more.

Navigating Spokeo's interface allows users to explore not only the primary subject of their search but also related individuals and associated addresses.

The interface provides tabs or sections for each category of information, making it easy for users to access specific details of interest.

For example, users can click on the "Family Members" tab to view a list of the subject's known relatives and their contact information.

Similarly, the "Addresses" tab provides information about the subject's current and previous residences, helping users understand their geographic history.

Spokeo's interface also offers a "Map" feature that allows users to visualize the subject's address locations on a map.

This feature is particularly useful for geolocation purposes, enabling OSINT practitioners to understand the subject's movements and connections to specific areas.

Spokeo's interface goes beyond individual profiles and addresses by providing insights into social media activity.

The interface can display a subject's recent social media posts, photos, and comments, offering a glimpse into their online presence and interactions.

This feature can be valuable for OSINT investigations involving online behavior and social connections.

The "Criminal Records" section of Spokeo's interface allows users to access information about a subject's criminal history, including any arrests, convictions, or offenses on their record.

This information can be crucial for background checks and investigative purposes.

Spokeo's interface also includes a "Reverse Phone" lookup feature, allowing users to enter a phone number and retrieve information about the associated individual or address.

This feature is particularly useful for identifying unknown callers or verifying the legitimacy of a phone contact.

Spokeo's interface provides various filters and search options to refine and customize results.

Users can narrow down their searches by location, age, and other criteria to focus on the most relevant information.

These filtering options enhance the precision of OSINT investigations and help users extract specific details from the interface.

Spokeo's interface is designed to be accessible from both desktop and mobile devices, ensuring that users can conduct investigations on the go.

The responsive design adapts to different screen sizes, making it convenient for OSINT practitioners who require flexibility in their research activities.

It's important to note that while Spokeo's interface offers valuable information, it is subject to limitations.

Certain details may be restricted or unavailable due to privacy settings, legal regulations, or data sources' restrictions.

Additionally, the accuracy of information retrieved from Spokeo's interface should always be verified through additional sources to ensure its reliability.

In summary, Spokeo's interface is a powerful tool for OSINT practitioners and investigators seeking to gather open-source information about individuals, organizations, and addresses.

Understanding how to navigate and utilize the interface effectively enables users to access comprehensive profiles, social media insights, criminal records, and more.

By using Spokeo's interface as part of their investigative toolkit, OSINT practitioners can enhance their ability to gather valuable intelligence and support various investigative objectives.

Basic searches and data interpretation are foundational skills for any OSINT practitioner seeking to extract valuable information from open sources.

These skills are essential for understanding how to effectively conduct searches, retrieve relevant data, and make sense of the information collected.

To begin with, basic searches involve using search engines, online databases, and other tools to query open-source information.

Search engines like Google, Bing, and Yahoo are often the first step in an OSINT investigation, as they provide access to a vast array of web content.

Using these search engines effectively requires knowing how to construct precise queries using keywords, operators, and filters.

Operators such as "AND," "OR," and "NOT" can be used to refine search results, ensuring that they are relevant to the investigation.

Moreover, quotation marks can be employed to search for exact phrases, while asterisks serve as wildcards to expand search possibilities.

Learning how to utilize advanced search operators and modifiers is an essential aspect of mastering basic searches in OSINT.

Additionally, OSINT practitioners should be aware of specialized search engines and online databases that cater to specific niches or industries.

For instance, academic researchers may use platforms like Google Scholar, while investigators focused on social media may utilize tools like Facebook Graph Search or Twitter Advanced Search.

Each of these tools offers unique features and search capabilities, and understanding their nuances can significantly enhance an OSINT practitioner's search capabilities.

As OSINT practitioners conduct basic searches, they will inevitably retrieve a multitude of results.

The ability to interpret and assess the relevance and credibility of these results is a critical skill.

Data interpretation involves scrutinizing search results to identify pertinent information while filtering out noise or irrelevant content.

One key consideration in data interpretation is the source of the information.

OSINT practitioners must evaluate the credibility and trustworthiness of the sources they encounter.

For instance, information from reputable news outlets, government websites, and academic publications generally carries more weight than content from anonymous forums or unverified blogs.

Cross-referencing information from multiple sources can help confirm its accuracy and reliability.

Another aspect of data interpretation is understanding the context in which information is presented.

Information can be manipulated or taken out of context, so it's crucial to consider the broader narrative surrounding a particular piece of data.

Analyzing the publication date of content is also essential to ensure the information is current and relevant to the investigation.

Outdated or obsolete information can lead to inaccurate conclusions.

Furthermore, basic searches often yield a mix of primary and secondary sources.

Distinguishing between these types of sources is important.

Primary sources provide original, firsthand information, while secondary sources offer interpretations or summaries of primary data.

OSINT practitioners should prioritize primary sources when available, as they tend to be more reliable.

When interpreting data from primary sources, it's important to consider the motivations and biases of the individuals or organizations providing the information.

Bias can impact the way information is presented and may influence the OSINT practitioner's understanding of the data.

Furthermore, metadata plays a crucial role in data interpretation.

Metadata includes information about the data itself, such as when it was created, who created it, and how it has been modified.

Analyzing metadata can provide insights into the origin and authenticity of the data.

Metadata can be found in various types of digital files, such as documents, images, and videos.

OSINT practitioners should be proficient in extracting and analyzing metadata to enhance their data interpretation skills.

In some cases, data interpretation may require linguistic or cultural knowledge.

Understanding the language and culture associated with the open-source information being analyzed can help interpret nuances, idioms, and cultural references.

Moreover, data interpretation involves organizing and structuring information in a way that supports the overall investigative objectives.

This may include creating timelines, charts, or graphs to visualize connections and patterns within the data.

Furthermore, OSINT practitioners should be mindful of the ethical considerations surrounding data interpretation.

Respecting individuals' privacy and consent when interpreting information is paramount.

Data interpretation should adhere to legal and ethical guidelines to ensure responsible and ethical OSINT practices.

In summary, basic searches and data interpretation are fundamental skills for OSINT practitioners.

Mastering these skills involves effectively using search engines and online databases to query open sources, constructing precise search queries, and utilizing advanced search operators and modifiers.

Data interpretation requires assessing the credibility of sources, considering context, evaluating the reliability of information, and analyzing metadata.

Additionally, understanding the linguistic and cultural aspects of the data and respecting ethical guidelines are essential components of data interpretation in OSINT.

Chapter 4: Spokeo Mastery for OSINT Ninjas

Advanced Spokeo search techniques enable OSINT practitioners to harness the full potential of this powerful tool for open-source intelligence investigations.

By delving deeper into the features and functionalities of Spokeo, practitioners can uncover valuable insights and information that may not be immediately apparent through basic searches.

One advanced technique in Spokeo is the use of advanced search operators and modifiers.

These operators allow practitioners to refine their queries further and narrow down the search results to pinpoint specific information.

For example, the "AND" operator can be used to combine multiple keywords, ensuring that search results include both terms.

Conversely, the "OR" operator broadens the search by including results containing either of the specified terms.

The "NOT" operator excludes specific terms from the search results, helping eliminate irrelevant information.

Utilizing these operators strategically enhances the precision of Spokeo searches.

Moreover, practitioners can employ quotation marks to search for exact phrases within Spokeo.

This feature is particularly valuable when seeking information related to specific names, addresses, or keywords.

By enclosing a phrase in quotation marks, Spokeo will only return results that match the exact phrase, increasing the relevance of the information retrieved.

Wildcard characters, such as asterisks, can also be used in Spokeo searches.

An asterisk serves as a placeholder for one or more characters, allowing practitioners to search for variations of a keyword.

For example, searching for "John * Smith" can yield results for variations like "John A. Smith" or "John Robert Smith."

In addition to advanced search operators, Spokeo offers search filters that enable practitioners to refine results based on specific criteria.

These filters can be applied to narrow down the search by location, age, gender, or even associated family members.

By using filters strategically, practitioners can tailor their searches to meet the unique requirements of their investigations.

Furthermore, Spokeo allows for reverse phone lookups, a powerful technique for identifying individuals or addresses associated with a particular phone number.

This feature is invaluable for verifying the legitimacy of phone contacts or uncovering hidden connections.

Reverse phone lookups can reveal the name, location, and potentially other information about the owner of a phone number.

Another advanced Spokeo search technique involves exploring the "Associations" section of the search results.

This section provides insights into the subject's potential affiliations or connections with organizations, groups, or networks.

It can help practitioners uncover valuable leads and understand the subject's social or professional associations.

The "Social Media" section of Spokeo's search results is another goldmine of information for OSINT practitioners.

This section provides links to the subject's social media profiles, including Facebook, Twitter, LinkedIn, Instagram, and more.

Exploring these profiles can reveal valuable insights into the subject's online presence, interests, connections, and activities.

OSINT practitioners can analyze social media posts, photos, comments, and interactions to gather intelligence.

Furthermore, Spokeo's "Criminal Records" section offers access to information about a subject's criminal history.

This section can be crucial for background checks and investigations requiring knowledge of an individual's legal past.

Practitioners can uncover details such as arrests, convictions, and offenses on the subject's record.

The "Maps" feature in Spokeo allows practitioners to visualize the subject's address locations on a map.

Geolocation is a powerful OSINT technique that helps track an individual's movements, identify connections to specific areas, or verify addresses.

By using the map feature, practitioners can gain valuable spatial insights.

Additionally, Spokeo's interface provides an option to export search results.

This feature allows practitioners to save and analyze data offline or share it with colleagues or clients.

Exporting results can be particularly useful when conducting in-depth investigations or building comprehensive reports.

OSINT practitioners should also take advantage of Spokeo's "Data Source" information.

Each result in Spokeo includes details about the sources from which the information was obtained.

Understanding the source of the data can help practitioners assess its credibility and reliability.

By cross-referencing data from multiple sources, practitioners can corroborate information and ensure its accuracy.

Finally, practitioners should consider the ethical implications of their advanced Spokeo searches.

Respecting privacy rights, obtaining consent when necessary, and avoiding deceptive practices are essential principles in responsible OSINT.

Advanced Spokeo search techniques are powerful tools in the OSINT practitioner's toolkit.

Mastering these techniques enables practitioners to conduct thorough investigations, uncover hidden information, and extract valuable intelligence from open sources.

By combining advanced search operators, filters, reverse phone lookups, and a deep dive into various sections of Spokeo's search results, practitioners can enhance their ability to achieve investigative objectives while adhering to ethical guidelines.

Leveraging Spokeo for deep reconnaissance is an advanced OSINT technique that allows investigators to uncover extensive information about individuals, organizations, or addresses.

Deep reconnaissance goes beyond basic searches and delves into the wealth of data that can be extracted from Spokeo's extensive database.

To effectively leverage Spokeo for deep reconnaissance, OSINT practitioners should begin by defining their research objectives and the scope of their investigation.

Clear objectives provide a roadmap for the reconnaissance process and help practitioners stay focused on gathering relevant information.

Once the objectives are established, practitioners can proceed to create a detailed search strategy.

This strategy should include specific search queries, keywords, and criteria that align with the research goals.

It's important to consider what type of information is needed, such as contact details, family connections, social media profiles, or criminal records.

The search strategy should also take into account any filters or advanced search operators that can be used to refine the results.

One of the key aspects of deep reconnaissance using Spokeo is the systematic exploration of search results.

Practitioners should carefully review each profile and entry to extract valuable information.

Profiles often contain a wealth of data, including names, addresses, phone numbers, email addresses, and more.

By examining this information closely, practitioners can build a comprehensive picture of the subject.

The "Associations" section within Spokeo's search results is a valuable resource for deep reconnaissance.

This section provides insights into the subject's potential affiliations, connections, or memberships in organizations, groups, or networks.

It can help practitioners uncover hidden associations and understand the subject's social or professional connections.

Furthermore, practitioners should explore the "Social Media" section within Spokeo's search results.

This section provides links to the subject's social media profiles, including Facebook, Twitter, LinkedIn, Instagram, and others.

Analyzing these profiles can yield valuable insights into the subject's online presence, interests, connections, and activities.

Practitioners can review social media posts, photos, comments, and interactions to gather intelligence.

Additionally, the "Criminal Records" section of Spokeo's search results is essential for deep reconnaissance.

This section offers access to information about a subject's criminal history, including arrests, convictions, and offenses on their record.

Understanding a subject's legal past can be crucial for certain investigations or background checks.

Geolocation plays a vital role in deep reconnaissance using Spokeo.

The "Maps" feature allows practitioners to visualize the subject's address locations on a map.

This capability helps track an individual's movements, identify connections to specific areas, or verify addresses.

Practitioners can use geolocation to gain valuable spatial insights during their reconnaissance.

Another valuable aspect of deep reconnaissance is cross-referencing information from multiple sources.

Spokeo provides details about the sources of the data, and practitioners should use this information to assess the credibility and reliability of the data.

Cross-referencing data ensures its accuracy and helps validate the information obtained.

Furthermore, Spokeo's "Data Source" information can be used to understand the origin of the data.

This information is critical for evaluating the credibility of the sources and the reliability of the data.

Ethical considerations are paramount in deep reconnaissance.

Practitioners should always respect privacy rights, obtain consent when necessary, and adhere to ethical principles throughout the investigation.

Deep reconnaissance using Spokeo can reveal a vast amount of information, but it must be conducted responsibly and ethically.

OSINT practitioners should also consider the legal implications of their reconnaissance activities.

Laws regarding data collection, privacy, and consent vary by jurisdiction, and practitioners should be aware of and compliant with relevant laws and regulations.

In summary, leveraging Spokeo for deep reconnaissance is a valuable skill for OSINT practitioners.

By defining clear objectives, creating a comprehensive search strategy, and systematically exploring search results, practitioners can gather extensive information about subjects, organizations, or addresses.

The use of advanced search operators, filters, and sections within Spokeo's search results enhances the depth and precision of reconnaissance.

Practitioners should also consider ethical and legal considerations to ensure responsible and lawful reconnaissance practices.

Chapter 5: Unraveling Spiderfoot's Beginner Techniques

Getting started with Spiderfoot is the first step toward harnessing the power of this comprehensive OSINT tool.

Spiderfoot is a versatile open-source reconnaissance tool that enables investigators to gather a wide range of information from various online sources.

Before diving into Spiderfoot, it's essential to understand its purpose and capabilities.

Spiderfoot is designed to automate the process of collecting data from websites, search engines, social media platforms, DNS servers, and other online sources.

It can be used for a variety of OSINT activities, including reconnaissance, threat intelligence, and cybersecurity investigations.

To begin using Spiderfoot, practitioners should start by downloading and installing the tool on their system.

Spiderfoot provides installation instructions on its official website, ensuring a smooth setup process.

Once Spiderfoot is installed, practitioners can access the tool through their web browser, as it operates as a web-based application.

The first step in Spiderfoot is to create a new scan.

A scan in Spiderfoot is an OSINT investigation focused on a specific target, such as an individual, organization, domain, or IP address.

Practitioners can give the scan a name and provide a brief description to keep track of their investigations.

After creating a new scan, practitioners need to define the target they want to investigate.

Spiderfoot supports various target types, including domain names, IP addresses, email addresses, phone numbers, and usernames.

The choice of target type depends on the nature of the investigation.

For example, if the goal is to gather information about a website, a domain name or IP address can be used as the target.

Practitioners can also specify the depth of the scan, which determines how far Spiderfoot will crawl the web to collect information.

Choosing a suitable depth ensures that the scan gathers relevant data without overwhelming the user with unnecessary information.

Once the target and scan depth are defined, practitioners can configure modules in Spiderfoot.

Modules are individual components that perform specific tasks during the scan.

Spiderfoot offers a wide range of modules, each designed to extract specific types of information.

For example, there are modules for DNS information, WHOIS data, social media profiles, email addresses, and more.

Practitioners can select the modules that are most relevant to their investigation and enable them for the scan.

Spiderfoot also allows practitioners to customize the configuration of each module, providing flexibility in data collection.

After configuring the modules, practitioners can initiate the scan.

Spiderfoot will start gathering data from the specified sources and modules.

The scan progress can be monitored in real-time through the Spiderfoot interface.

As the scan progresses, practitioners can view the collected data, organized into categories such as Hostnames, URLs, Email Addresses, and more.

Spiderfoot provides a summary of the collected information, making it easy to assess the results of the scan.

One of the advantages of Spiderfoot is its ability to integrate with external data sources.

Practitioners can configure Spiderfoot to fetch additional data from external APIs and services, enriching the investigation.

External data sources may include threat intelligence feeds, geolocation services, and reputation databases.

By incorporating external data, practitioners can enhance the depth and accuracy of their OSINT investigations.

Spiderfoot also allows practitioners to export the results of their scans in various formats, including CSV, JSON, and HTML.

Exporting the data enables practitioners to create reports, share findings with colleagues or clients, or analyze the information further using external tools.

Another useful feature of Spiderfoot is its scheduling capabilities.

Practitioners can schedule scans to run at specific intervals automatically.

This feature is valuable for continuous monitoring and threat intelligence gathering.

It ensures that practitioners stay updated with the latest information related to their targets.

Security and privacy are critical considerations when using Spiderfoot.

Practitioners should ensure that they have the necessary permissions to conduct scans on the chosen targets.

Additionally, it's essential to respect the terms of service and legal regulations of the sources being queried.

Failure to do so may result in legal consequences or the termination of access to certain data sources.

In summary, getting started with Spiderfoot is the initial phase of an OSINT investigation.

Understanding Spiderfoot's purpose, installing the tool, defining targets, configuring modules, and initiating scans are the essential steps in the process.

Practitioners can leverage Spiderfoot's capabilities, integration with external data sources, and scheduling features to conduct comprehensive OSINT investigations efficiently.

By following ethical and legal guidelines, practitioners can use Spiderfoot to gather valuable intelligence while respecting privacy and data source regulations.

Basic reconnaissance with Spiderfoot is the foundation of any OSINT investigation, providing valuable insights into a target's online presence.

This phase involves initial data collection and the identification of key information sources.

To begin, practitioners should have a clear understanding of their investigation's objectives and the specific target they intend to analyze using Spiderfoot.

Once the target is defined, practitioners can initiate a basic reconnaissance scan within Spiderfoot.

The scan setup involves specifying the target's type, such as a domain name, IP address, email address, or username.

The choice of target type depends on the nature of the investigation and the available information about the target.

Practitioners can also select the scan depth, which determines the extent to which Spiderfoot will explore online sources.

Choosing an appropriate scan depth is crucial, as it ensures the scan's focus remains relevant to the investigation.

Once the target and scan depth are configured, practitioners can proceed to select the appropriate modules for the scan.

Spiderfoot provides a wide range of modules, each designed to extract specific types of information from online sources.

For instance, modules can be chosen for collecting DNS information, WHOIS data, email addresses, social media profiles, and more.

Selecting relevant modules is essential, as they determine the types of data collected during the reconnaissance phase.

Spiderfoot allows practitioners to customize the configuration of each module to tailor data collection to their specific needs.

After configuring the modules, practitioners can initiate the reconnaissance scan.

Spiderfoot will begin collecting data from the specified sources and modules.

The scan's progress can be monitored in real-time through Spiderfoot's user interface, providing immediate insights into the data being gathered.

As the scan progresses, the collected information is organized into categories, making it easier for practitioners to review and analyze the results.

Spiderfoot provides a summary of the collected data, offering a high-level view of the initial reconnaissance findings.

One valuable feature of Spiderfoot is its ability to integrate with external data sources.

Practitioners can configure Spiderfoot to fetch additional data from external APIs and services, enriching the investigation.

These external sources may include threat intelligence feeds, geolocation services, and reputation databases.

By incorporating external data, practitioners can enhance the depth and context of their reconnaissance results.

Once the reconnaissance scan is completed, practitioners have the option to export the gathered data in various formats, such as CSV, JSON, or HTML.

Exporting the data enables practitioners to create comprehensive reports, share findings with team members or clients, or further analyze the information using external tools.

Additionally, Spiderfoot offers scheduling capabilities, allowing practitioners to automate scans at specific intervals.

Scheduled scans are useful for continuous monitoring and keeping investigations up-to-date.

They ensure that practitioners remain informed about any changes or developments related to their targets.

Security and privacy considerations are essential throughout the basic reconnaissance phase.

Practitioners must ensure that they have the necessary permissions to conduct scans on the chosen targets.

Respecting the terms of service and legal regulations of the data sources being queried is paramount to avoid legal consequences.

Practitioners should also be mindful of ethical principles, including obtaining consent when necessary and respecting individuals' privacy.

In summary, basic reconnaissance with Spiderfoot is a fundamental step in any OSINT investigation.

It involves setting clear objectives, configuring the scan for the target and scan depth, selecting relevant modules, and initiating the scan.

Monitoring the scan's progress, organizing collected data, and exporting results are crucial aspects of the reconnaissance process.

Integration with external data sources, scheduling scans, and adhering to security, privacy, and ethical considerations further enhance the effectiveness of basic reconnaissance with Spiderfoot.

Ultimately, this phase provides the initial foundation of intelligence upon which subsequent investigation steps can be built.

Chapter 6: Spiderfoot's Advanced Ninja Strategies

Advanced Spiderfoot modules and customization are key elements of mastering this powerful OSINT tool, allowing practitioners to tailor their investigations and gather highly specific intelligence.

These advanced modules extend Spiderfoot's functionality beyond basic reconnaissance, enabling practitioners to delve deeper into their targets' digital footprints.

To harness the full potential of Spiderfoot's advanced modules, it's crucial to understand their capabilities and how to customize them effectively.

One advanced module is the "Social Media Footprint" module, which focuses on collecting information from various social media platforms.

By enabling this module, practitioners can gather data from platforms like Facebook, Twitter, LinkedIn, Instagram, and others associated with the target.

This provides insights into the target's online presence, connections, and activities across social media.

The "Pwned Passwords" module is another advanced feature, allowing practitioners to check if a target's email addresses or usernames have been compromised in data breaches.

Enabling this module enhances cybersecurity investigations by identifying potential security risks.

Customization is a critical aspect of using advanced modules effectively.

Practitioners can adjust module configurations to refine data collection, ensuring that the results align with their investigation objectives.

Customization options may include specifying keywords, domains, or sources to focus on during the scan.

For example, in the "Social Media Footprint" module, practitioners can input specific social media handles or domains to target, narrowing the scope of data collection.

Another advanced module, "DarkWeb Marketplaces," enables practitioners to investigate whether target email addresses or usernames have appeared in listings on dark web marketplaces.

This module is particularly valuable for cybersecurity and threat intelligence investigations.

Customization options allow practitioners to specify which dark web marketplaces to monitor, tailoring the module to their research needs.

The "Threat Intelligence Feeds" module integrates external threat intelligence sources into Spiderfoot scans.

Practitioners can configure this module to retrieve information from various threat intelligence feeds, enhancing the reconnaissance process with up-to-date threat data.

Customization options enable practitioners to select specific feeds and filter the data based on relevance.

Advanced Spiderfoot modules also include "Company Information," which provides insights into a target organization's online presence, including domains, IP addresses, and associated entities.

Customization options for this module allow practitioners to focus on specific companies or industries, streamlining corporate intelligence efforts.

Another powerful feature is the "Exposed Panels" module, which identifies instances where publicly accessible administration panels, such as login pages or control panels, are associated with a target's domain or IP address.

Customization options enable practitioners to refine the scan by specifying the types of panels to investigate.

In addition to these modules, Spiderfoot offers "Geolocation" capabilities, allowing practitioners to pinpoint the physical location associated with a target.

This module can be used to track IP addresses or domain names to specific geographical coordinates.

Customization options include specifying the type of geolocation data to collect, such as city, country, or latitude and longitude.

Furthermore, practitioners can explore the "Custom Search Engine" module, which enables them to create custom search queries tailored to their investigation objectives.

This module offers flexibility in data collection by allowing practitioners to define specific search criteria and sources.

Customization options within the "Custom Search Engine" module are extensive, including the ability to craft complex search strings and select preferred search engines.

To use advanced modules effectively, practitioners should regularly update Spiderfoot to access the latest features and improvements.

Additionally, they should stay informed about new external data sources, threat intelligence feeds, and dark web marketplaces to incorporate into their investigations.

Security and privacy considerations remain paramount when utilizing advanced modules.

Practitioners must ensure that their scans comply with legal regulations and ethical guidelines.

Respecting privacy rights, obtaining consent when necessary, and adhering to data source terms of service are critical practices.

Customization should be carried out thoughtfully to avoid overloading scans with irrelevant data.

The selection of specific modules and customization options should align closely with the investigation's goals.

In summary, advanced Spiderfoot modules and customization empower OSINT practitioners to conduct in-depth investigations and gather highly specific intelligence.

By leveraging features like the "Social Media Footprint," "Pwned Passwords," "DarkWeb Marketplaces," and others, practitioners can refine their scans and extract valuable insights.

Customization options within these modules allow practitioners to tailor data collection to their research objectives, increasing the precision and relevance of their findings.

However, practitioners should always prioritize security, privacy, and ethical considerations when using advanced modules, ensuring responsible and lawful OSINT practices.

Ninja-level intelligence gathering with Spiderfoot represents the pinnacle of OSINT expertise, enabling practitioners to uncover hidden insights, connections, and secrets with unparalleled precision and depth.

To attain this level of mastery, practitioners must not only understand Spiderfoot's advanced features but also possess a deep comprehension of their investigation's goals and targets.

At this stage, practitioners can wield Spiderfoot as a finely tuned instrument, extracting intelligence that eludes others.

The journey to ninja-level intelligence gathering begins by formulating clear objectives and defining the scope of the investigation.

Without a well-defined purpose, practitioners risk wandering aimlessly through the vast landscape of online information.

Once the objectives are crystal clear, practitioners can proceed to create an intricate web of interconnected scans within Spiderfoot.

This web of scans represents a holistic approach to intelligence gathering, encompassing a wide array of target types, sources, and modules.

The selection of targets is strategic, covering various aspects of the investigation, such as individuals, organizations, domains, IP addresses, and more.

Each target type may require a distinct set of modules and customizations to extract the most relevant data.

Practitioners may choose to investigate associations between targets, exploring how different entities are interconnected.

This approach helps uncover hidden relationships, dependencies, or affiliations that can be crucial in complex investigations.

To achieve ninja-level intelligence gathering, practitioners should leverage Spiderfoot's advanced modules, including those focused on social media, dark web marketplaces, threat intelligence feeds, and company information.

These modules serve as the foundation for deep reconnaissance, offering insights that extend beyond the surface-level data available through basic scans.

Customization at this level becomes an art form, allowing practitioners to fine-tune module configurations with surgical precision.

Keywords, search criteria, sources, and filters are meticulously chosen to align with the investigation's goals.

The ability to craft intricate search queries and harness the full potential of external data sources sets ninja-level practitioners apart.

They possess a deep understanding of the sources they query, knowing which ones are reliable, authoritative, or prone to misinformation.

Furthermore, ninja-level intelligence gatherers master the art of data enrichment by seamlessly integrating external data sources into their scans.

These sources provide a real-time stream of threat intelligence, geolocation data, and dark web insights, enhancing the depth and currency of their findings.

Cross-referencing data from multiple sources becomes second nature, allowing practitioners to validate information and build a comprehensive intelligence picture.

For example, correlating social media profiles, email addresses, and dark web mentions can reveal hidden connections and patterns.

Spiderfoot's geolocation capabilities are harnessed to their fullest extent, enabling practitioners to trace the physical locations associated with targets.

This geospatial intelligence provides a critical dimension to investigations, especially when tracking the movements or activities of individuals or organizations.

Ninja-level intelligence gatherers excel in identifying and analyzing exposed panels or vulnerable web applications associated with their targets.

This skill extends beyond basic reconnaissance and requires an in-depth understanding of web security and attack vectors.

By pinpointing potential vulnerabilities, practitioners can advise on remediation measures or exploit security weaknesses for legitimate purposes.

The integration of machine learning and advanced analytics tools elevates ninja-level intelligence gathering to new heights.

Practitioners harness these technologies to sift through vast amounts of data, identify patterns, anomalies, and trends, and distill actionable intelligence.

Machine learning models can automate the analysis of text, images, and other forms of unstructured data, uncovering hidden insights.

Ethical considerations remain paramount at the ninja level.

Practitioners must navigate a complex landscape of legal and ethical challenges, respecting privacy rights, obtaining consent when necessary, and adhering to data source terms of service.

They are acutely aware of the potential impact of their intelligence gathering activities on individuals, organizations, and society as a whole.

Moreover, ninja-level intelligence gatherers possess a deep understanding of the legal implications of their actions.

They are well-versed in the laws governing data collection, privacy, and cybersecurity, ensuring compliance with regional and international regulations.

In summary, ninja-level intelligence gathering with Spiderfoot represents the zenith of OSINT expertise.

It is characterized by a profound understanding of Spiderfoot's advanced features, a strategic approach to investigations, and an unwavering commitment to ethical and legal principles.

Practitioners at this level wield Spiderfoot as a precision instrument, extracting intelligence with unmatched precision and depth.

Their ability to customize module configurations, integrate external data sources, cross-reference information, and leverage machine learning sets them apart as true OSINT ninjas.

While the journey to ninja-level intelligence gathering is arduous, it yields invaluable insights, connections, and secrets that can make a profound impact in the world of intelligence and investigations.

Chapter 7: SEON: A Novice's Guide to Open-Source Intelligence

Introduction to SEON and its features provides a foundational understanding of this powerful open-source intelligence tool, enabling practitioners to harness its capabilities effectively.

SEON, short for Search Engine Operator Ninja, is a versatile and comprehensive OSINT tool that specializes in harnessing the power of search engines to gather intelligence.

As a command-line tool, SEON is designed for advanced users who are comfortable working in a terminal environment.

SEON's primary strength lies in its ability to execute complex search queries across multiple search engines and online platforms.

This enables practitioners to access a wealth of information that may not be readily available through conventional search methods.

One of SEON's standout features is its extensive list of search engine operators.

Search engine operators are specialized commands that allow practitioners to refine and focus their search queries.

SEON provides a vast array of operators, each tailored to extract specific types of information or target particular online sources.

These operators include site-specific queries, file type filters, domain searches, and more.

Practitioners can combine multiple operators to create highly customized search queries that suit their investigation objectives.

SEON also supports the use of custom search engines, giving practitioners the flexibility to define their own search sources.

This feature is particularly valuable when dealing with niche or specialized online platforms that may not be covered by traditional search engines.

Custom search engines can be configured in SEON to target specific websites, forums, or databases, expanding the scope of the OSINT investigation.

In addition to search engine operators and custom search engines, SEON offers advanced filtering capabilities.

Practitioners can apply filters to their search results to refine and sort the information based on various criteria.

These filters can be used to focus on specific file types, dates, languages, and more, allowing practitioners to pinpoint the most relevant results.

SEON's support for proxies and user agents enhances privacy and anonymity during OSINT investigations. Practitioners can configure SEON to route their search queries through proxy servers and emulate different user agents to avoid detection or tracking. This is particularly important when conducting sensitive or covert investigations. Another noteworthy feature of SEON is its support for scripting and automation. Practitioners can create scripts to automate repetitive search tasks and execute them through SEON's command-line interface.

This automation capability saves time and ensures consistency in gathering intelligence across multiple sessions. SEON's scripting language is versatile, allowing practitioners to create complex workflows tailored to their specific needs.

Furthermore, SEON provides the option to export search results in various formats, such as CSV, JSON, or HTML. Exporting results facilitates the creation of detailed reports, sharing findings with colleagues, or further analysis using external tools.

While SEON is a powerful tool, it requires a certain level of technical proficiency to operate effectively.

Practitioners should be familiar with command-line interfaces, search engine operators, and scripting languages to maximize SEON's potential.

Security and privacy considerations are essential when using SEON.

Practitioners should be mindful of their digital footprint and take precautions to protect their identity during OSINT investigations.

SEON's support for proxies and user agents helps mitigate potential risks, but practitioners should also be aware of legal and ethical boundaries.

Respecting the terms of service of search engines and websites is crucial to avoid legal repercussions.

In summary, SEON is a robust OSINT tool designed for advanced users who seek to harness the full power of search engines in their investigations.

Its extensive list of search engine operators, support for custom search engines, advanced filtering capabilities, privacy features, and scripting options make it a valuable asset for OSINT practitioners.

However, proficiency in command-line interfaces, scripting, and a strong understanding of security and privacy considerations are prerequisites for effectively using SEON in OSINT investigations.

With the right knowledge and skills, practitioners can leverage SEON to uncover valuable intelligence and insights from the vast expanse of online information.

Beginner investigations with SEON mark the initial steps into the world of open-source intelligence, offering newcomers an accessible entry point to explore the tool's capabilities.

SEON's command-line interface may appear daunting at first, but with a gradual approach, beginners can quickly grasp its fundamental concepts and functionalities.

The primary goal of beginner-level SEON investigations is to gain familiarity with the tool's command structure, search operators, and basic search techniques.

To begin, practitioners should open a terminal or command prompt on their computer and navigate to the directory where SEON is installed.

The first command to become acquainted with is the "seon" command itself, which serves as the entry point for launching SEON.

Typing "seon" in the terminal and pressing enter will initiate the tool and display the SEON prompt, indicating that the tool is ready for commands.

An essential command for beginners is the "help" command, which provides access to SEON's built-in documentation.

Typing "help" followed by a specific command or operator, such as "help search," will display information about that particular command or operator, including its usage and options.

Beginners should take the time to explore SEON's help documentation to understand the available commands and their functionalities.

Once practitioners have a basic understanding of the command structure, they can start experimenting with simple search queries.

The "search" command is fundamental, and it allows users to initiate search queries across various search engines and online platforms.

To perform a basic search, practitioners can use the following command: "search [query]." For example, "search Open-source intelligence."

SEON will execute the query and display the results directly in the terminal.

At this stage, beginners can become acquainted with the concept of search engine operators, which enhance the precision of search queries.

Operators are keywords or symbols that modify search queries to target specific types of information or sources.

For instance, the "site:" operator restricts the search to a particular website or domain, while the "filetype:" operator filters results by file type.

Beginners can practice using operators in their search queries, such as "search site:wikipedia.org OSINT" to search specifically within Wikipedia.

Additionally, SEON supports Boolean operators, allowing practitioners to combine keywords and operators for more complex searches.

The "AND," "OR," and "NOT" operators are commonly used to refine search results further.

For example, "search OSINT AND cybersecurity" will return results related to both OSINT and cybersecurity.

Beginners can experiment with Boolean operators to understand how they influence search outcomes.

As beginners gain confidence in crafting search queries, they can explore SEON's capabilities further.

The "settings" command provides access to various configuration options, allowing practitioners to customize SEON to their preferences.

For example, practitioners can set their default search engine, configure proxy settings for enhanced privacy, and adjust output formatting options.

While conducting beginner investigations, it's essential to be mindful of ethical considerations and legal boundaries.

Practitioners should adhere to the terms of service of search engines and websites and respect individuals' privacy rights.

SEON's proxy support can help anonymize searches, but practitioners should remain aware of the potential legal and ethical implications of their actions.

In summary, beginner investigations with SEON offer a valuable introduction to the world of open-source intelligence.

Practitioners can start by becoming familiar with SEON's command structure, help documentation, and fundamental commands.

Experimenting with basic search queries and search engine operators provides hands-on experience in harnessing SEON's capabilities.

As practitioners progress, they can explore more advanced features, such as configuration options and Boolean operators, to refine their investigative skills.

Throughout their journey, practitioners should prioritize ethical and legal considerations to conduct responsible and lawful OSINT investigations.

Chapter 8: SEON Expertise: Advanced OSINT Tactics

Mastering SEON's advanced capabilities represents a significant milestone for open-source intelligence practitioners, allowing them to elevate their investigative skills to an elite level.

At this stage, practitioners should have a solid understanding of SEON's command-line interface, basic search queries, and search engine operators.

Building on this foundation, they can delve into the tool's more sophisticated features and techniques.

One of the key aspects of mastering SEON is gaining proficiency in crafting complex search queries that leverage advanced operators.

The "site:" operator, which restricts searches to specific websites or domains, becomes a powerful tool in the hands of experienced practitioners.

For instance, by using "site:wikipedia.org," practitioners can focus their search exclusively on Wikipedia, a valuable source of information.

Additionally, SEON supports operators like "intitle:" and "inurl:" to target keywords within the titles or URLs of web pages, further refining search results.

For example, "intitle:cybersecurity" will yield results where the term "cybersecurity" appears in the titles of web pages.

Advanced operators such as "cache:" allow practitioners to access cached versions of web pages, enabling them to view content that may have been removed or updated.

By using "cache:[URL]," practitioners can retrieve the cached version of a specific web page.

SEON also provides support for the "filetype:" operator, which allows practitioners to filter results by file type.

This is particularly useful for locating specific documents, such as PDFs or spreadsheets.

By using "filetype:pdf," practitioners can target PDF documents in their searches.

Boolean operators, such as "AND," "OR," and "NOT," remain essential tools for advanced investigations.

Practitioners can combine multiple keywords and operators to construct intricate search queries.

For instance, "OSINT AND cybersecurity NOT social media" will return results related to OSINT and cybersecurity while excluding those related to social media.

Another advanced capability of SEON is its ability to search for specific file types within websites or domains.

The "site:[domain] filetype:[file type]" query can be used to target particular file types within a specific domain.

This can be valuable when seeking documents, presentations, or multimedia files on a particular website.

SEON's custom search engines feature allows practitioners to define their own search sources, expanding the tool's scope.

Practitioners can create custom search engines to target specific websites, forums, or databases that may not be covered by standard search engines.

By configuring custom search engines, practitioners gain access to unique and specialized sources of information.

Furthermore, SEON's scripting capabilities enable practitioners to automate and streamline their investigative workflows.

Scripts can be created to execute sequences of commands, perform repetitive tasks, and extract data from search results.

Advanced users can harness the power of scripting to save time and ensure consistency in their investigations.

The scripting language within SEON is versatile, allowing practitioners to create complex and customized automation routines.

Additionally, SEON provides the ability to export search results in various formats, facilitating the generation of detailed reports or further analysis using external tools.

Practitioners can use the "output" command to specify the format and location for exporting search results.

Common formats include CSV, JSON, and HTML, among others.

While mastering SEON's advanced capabilities opens up a wealth of opportunities for OSINT investigations, practitioners must remain vigilant about ethical and legal considerations.

Respecting the terms of service of search engines and websites is paramount to avoid violating their policies.

Practitioners should also be aware of the potential privacy implications of their actions, especially when dealing with sensitive or personal information.

In summary, mastering SEON's advanced capabilities represents a significant step in becoming an elite open-source intelligence practitioner.

Proficiency in crafting complex search queries, leveraging advanced operators, utilizing custom search engines, scripting automation, and exporting search results are skills that set advanced users apart.

However, practitioners must exercise ethical responsibility and legal compliance in their advanced investigations to ensure responsible and lawful OSINT practices.

Strategic SEON techniques for experts represent the pinnacle of open-source intelligence proficiency, enabling seasoned practitioners to conduct highly targeted and in-depth investigations.

At this advanced level, experts have honed their skills in crafting intricate search queries, utilizing advanced operators, and leveraging SEON's scripting capabilities.

They possess a deep understanding of SEON's inner workings and can navigate its command-line interface with ease.

Strategic SEON techniques are characterized by a strategic and purpose-driven approach to OSINT investigations.

Experts prioritize specific objectives and tailor their techniques to achieve precise outcomes.

One of the hallmarks of strategic SEON techniques is the ability to identify and target hidden or unconventional online sources.

Experts recognize that valuable intelligence can often be found in the less obvious corners of the internet.

For example, they may search through obscure forums, community websites, or niche online communities to uncover specialized knowledge or discussions.

Experts also leverage SEON's custom search engines extensively, creating highly specialized sources that cater to their investigation's unique requirements.

These custom search engines are finely tuned to focus on specific websites, databases, or forums that may not be indexed by mainstream search engines.

Through the use of custom search engines, experts expand their investigative reach and tap into a wealth of specialized knowledge.

Furthermore, experts are skilled in using SEON's advanced filtering options to sift through vast amounts of data efficiently.

They apply filters to narrow down search results based on criteria such as publication date, language, geographic location, and more.

This precision allows experts to extract the most relevant information quickly.

Additionally, experts have a keen eye for discerning patterns and trends within search results.

They utilize SEON's capabilities to perform advanced data analysis, identifying connections, anomalies, and correlations.

For instance, experts may cross-reference data from multiple sources, revealing hidden relationships between entities.

This cross-referencing can uncover valuable insights that would be missed through superficial analysis.

Strategic SEON techniques also involve a deep understanding of online information dynamics.

Experts are proficient in tracking the evolution of online content and identifying changes or updates over time.

They use SEON to access cached versions of web pages, preserving historical data that might have been altered or removed.

This historical perspective is crucial in piecing together a comprehensive intelligence picture.

Experts excel in integrating SEON with other OSINT tools and resources.

They understand how SEON can complement and enhance the capabilities of other tools, creating a powerful synergy.

For example, SEON can be used in conjunction with data visualization tools to create interactive maps or graphs that provide a visual representation of findings.

These visualizations offer a dynamic way to present complex information and insights.

In addition to advanced search techniques, experts are skilled in utilizing SEON's scripting and automation features to streamline their workflows.

They create intricate scripts that orchestrate sequences of commands, automate repetitive tasks, and extract data systematically.

These scripts save time and ensure consistency, allowing experts to focus on analysis and interpretation.

Moreover, experts are highly aware of the ethical considerations and legal implications of their investigations.

They adhere rigorously to ethical guidelines, respecting individuals' privacy and data protection rights.

Experts are also well-versed in the legal boundaries governing OSINT practices and ensure strict compliance with regional and international regulations.

A crucial aspect of strategic SEON techniques is the ability to deliver actionable intelligence.

Experts go beyond collecting information; they analyze, synthesize, and interpret data to provide actionable insights and recommendations.

They understand the importance of tailoring their findings to meet the specific needs of clients or organizations.

Furthermore, experts recognize the value of reporting and communication in OSINT investigations.

They prepare detailed and well-structured reports that convey findings clearly and concisely.

These reports are designed to be informative and accessible to both technical and non-technical stakeholders.

In summary, strategic SEON techniques for experts represent the highest level of open-source intelligence proficiency.

Experts excel in identifying and targeting hidden online sources, using custom search engines, applying advanced filtering and data analysis, and integrating SEON with other tools. Their ability to automate workflows, ensure ethical and legal compliance, and deliver actionable intelligence sets them apart as elite OSINT practitioners.

These experts approach each investigation with a strategic mindset, focused on achieving specific objectives and delivering valuable insights.

Chapter 9: Lampyre Basics and Beyond

The Lampyre interface and setup process serve as the gateway to harnessing the advanced capabilities of this powerful open-source intelligence tool.

Upon launching Lampyre, users are greeted with a user-friendly and intuitive interface that provides easy access to a wide range of OSINT features.

The interface is designed to facilitate efficient navigation and customization, ensuring that users can tailor their experience to meet their specific investigative needs.

To begin utilizing Lampyre, users need to install and configure the tool on their computer, which typically involves downloading the appropriate installer and following the installation instructions.

Once Lampyre is successfully installed, users can launch the application, and they will be presented with the main dashboard, which serves as the central hub for their OSINT activities.

The dashboard is divided into various panels, each dedicated to specific functionalities and tools, allowing users to organize their workflow efficiently.

Users have the flexibility to customize the layout of the dashboard, arranging panels to suit their preferences and workflow.

Lampyre offers users the ability to import data from various sources, enhancing the richness of their investigations.

Users can import data in various formats, including spreadsheets, CSV files, JSON, and more, making it easy to integrate external data into their OSINT operations.

This data import capability enables users to analyze and visualize information from diverse sources seamlessly.

The Lampyre interface also provides an array of built-in tools and modules that cover a broad spectrum of OSINT tasks.

These tools range from data collection and analysis to geospatial mapping and social media monitoring, offering users a comprehensive toolkit to conduct investigations effectively.

Lampyre's interface is designed with user-friendliness in mind, featuring intuitive drag-and-drop functionality for connecting modules and building investigation workflows.

Users can effortlessly construct data processing pipelines by dragging modules onto the canvas, connecting them, and configuring their settings.

This visual approach streamlines the process of building complex investigative workflows without requiring extensive technical expertise.

Furthermore, Lampyre offers powerful data visualization capabilities, allowing users to transform raw data into insightful visual representations.

Users can create charts, graphs, heatmaps, and interactive maps to gain a deeper understanding of their data and identify patterns and trends.

The interface provides a range of customization options for visualizations, enabling users to tailor them to their specific analytical needs.

Lampyre's interface also supports geospatial analysis, allowing users to visualize and explore geographic data.

Users can plot locations on maps, analyze spatial relationships, and perform geospatial queries to extract valuable insights from location-based information.

This feature is particularly valuable for investigations that involve mapping the activities and movements of individuals or organizations.

In addition to its powerful data processing and visualization capabilities, Lampyre offers users the option to export their findings in various formats.

Users can generate reports, export data in spreadsheet formats, save visualizations as images or interactive web applications, and share their insights with colleagues or stakeholders.

This export functionality ensures that the results of OSINT investigations can be effectively communicated and utilized for decision-making.

Lampyre's interface also supports collaboration among investigators, enabling multiple users to work together on the same investigation.

Users can share investigation workflows, data, and insights with team members, fostering a collaborative approach to OSINT operations.

Furthermore, Lampyre's interface is designed with a focus on user privacy and security.

The tool provides options for users to configure proxy settings, ensuring that their online activities remain anonymous and protected during investigations.

This feature is essential for maintaining confidentiality and discretion, particularly in sensitive or covert operations.

In summary, the Lampyre interface and setup process serve as the foundation for conducting sophisticated open-source intelligence investigations.

The user-friendly interface offers intuitive navigation, customization options, and powerful tools for data collection, analysis, visualization, and geospatial mapping.

Users can seamlessly import external data, construct investigation workflows, and export their findings in various formats.

Collaboration features and privacy safeguards make Lampyre a versatile and secure OSINT tool for a wide range of investigative needs.

Advanced data analysis with Lampyre is a crucial aspect of open-source intelligence (OSINT) investigations, enabling analysts to extract meaningful insights from vast and complex datasets.

Next, we will delve into the advanced techniques and methodologies used to analyze data effectively using Lampyre's powerful features.

Before diving into the specifics of data analysis, it is essential to understand the importance of data quality and preparation.

One of the initial steps in advanced data analysis is data cleansing, which involves identifying and rectifying errors, inconsistencies, and missing values in the dataset.

Lampyre provides tools to clean and preprocess data, ensuring that it is accurate and ready for analysis.

Once the data is cleaned, analysts can begin exploring it to gain a deeper understanding of its structure and content.

Lampyre's interface offers various data exploration capabilities, such as data profiling, summary statistics, and data visualization.

Analysts can generate summary reports, histograms, scatter plots, and other visualizations to uncover patterns and anomalies within the data.

These initial exploratory steps help analysts form hypotheses and guide their subsequent analysis.

Advanced data analysis often involves the application of statistical and mathematical techniques to derive insights from data.

Lampyre provides a wide range of statistical functions and libraries that analysts can leverage for in-depth analysis.

Analysts can perform statistical tests, regression analysis, hypothesis testing, and more to extract valuable information.

Additionally, Lampyre supports machine learning algorithms, allowing analysts to build predictive models and classification systems based on their data.

Machine learning can be particularly valuable in OSINT investigations for tasks such as sentiment analysis, entity recognition, and anomaly detection.

One of the essential aspects of advanced data analysis is data enrichment, which involves augmenting existing datasets with additional information from external sources.

Lampyre offers integration with numerous external data sources, enabling analysts to enrich their data with geospatial information, demographic data, social media activity, and more.

This enrichment process enhances the context and relevance of the data, making it more valuable for analysis.

Another critical aspect of data analysis with Lampyre is network analysis, which involves examining relationships and connections within datasets.

Lampyre provides tools for building and visualizing networks, allowing analysts to identify influencers, central nodes, and patterns of interaction.

Network analysis can be applied to various OSINT scenarios, including tracking criminal networks, identifying influencers in social media, and uncovering hidden relationships among entities.

Text analysis is another advanced data analysis technique supported by Lampyre.

Analysts can process and analyze text data, including web content, social media posts, emails, and documents, to extract insights, sentiment, and trends.

Text analysis tools within Lampyre enable the identification of keywords, sentiment analysis, topic modeling, and named entity recognition.

Analysts can use these techniques to uncover valuable information hidden within text data.

Temporal analysis is essential in OSINT investigations, as it involves the examination of data over time to identify trends, patterns, and anomalies.

Lampyre provides time series analysis capabilities, enabling analysts to visualize and analyze temporal data effectively.

Temporal analysis can be particularly valuable for tracking changes in online behavior, monitoring events, and identifying emerging trends.

In addition to the analytical tools mentioned earlier, Lampyre offers geospatial analysis features that are crucial for OSINT investigations.

Analysts can geocode data, plot locations on maps, and perform spatial queries to gain insights into geographic aspects of their investigations.

This is especially useful for tracking the movements of individuals or organizations, identifying geographic clusters, and visualizing geospatial patterns.

Collaboration and reporting are integral to advanced data analysis with Lampyre.

Analysts can share their analysis workflows, visualizations, and findings with colleagues and stakeholders within the Lampyre environment.

Furthermore, Lampyre supports the generation of comprehensive reports that summarize analysis results and insights for decision-makers.

Ethical considerations play a significant role in advanced data analysis within the context of OSINT investigations.

Analysts must adhere to ethical guidelines, respect privacy, and ensure that their analysis is conducted within legal boundaries.

Lampyre provides tools for data anonymization and compliance with data protection regulations, allowing analysts to conduct responsible and lawful investigations.

In summary, advanced data analysis with Lampyre empowers OSINT analysts to extract valuable insights from complex and diverse datasets.

Through data cleansing, exploration, statistical analysis, machine learning, enrichment, network analysis, text analysis, temporal analysis, and geospatial analysis, analysts can uncover hidden information, trends, and patterns.

Collaboration and reporting facilitate effective communication of findings, while ethical considerations ensure responsible and lawful analysis in OSINT investigations.

Chapter 10: Becoming an OSINT Ninja: Real-World Applications and Challenges

Real-world OSINT success stories provide tangible examples of how open-source intelligence has been instrumental in solving complex problems and uncovering critical information.

These stories showcase the practical application of OSINT techniques and the impact they can have in various domains.

One notable success story involves the identification of criminal activities through social media analysis.

In this case, law enforcement agencies used OSINT to track the activities of a criminal organization involved in drug trafficking.

By monitoring social media posts, analyzing online communications, and geolocating images, investigators were able to identify key individuals and gather evidence to support their case.

The insights gained from OSINT played a crucial role in dismantling the criminal network and securing convictions.

Another compelling OSINT success story revolves around the use of open-source intelligence in cybersecurity.

A cybersecurity firm leveraged OSINT techniques to uncover a sophisticated cyberattack targeting a multinational corporation.

By monitoring underground forums, analyzing malware samples, and tracking the attackers' infrastructure, the cybersecurity experts were able to attribute the attack to a nation-state actor.

This attribution allowed the victim organization to take appropriate defensive measures and mitigate the threat.

OSINT has also played a vital role in humanitarian efforts and disaster response.

In one instance, OSINT practitioners collaborated with humanitarian organizations to provide real-time information during a natural disaster.

Using social media monitoring, satellite imagery analysis, and geospatial data, they were able to identify affected areas, assess the extent of damage, and coordinate rescue and relief operations.

The timely and accurate information gathered through OSINT helped save lives and allocate resources effectively.

In the realm of business intelligence, OSINT has been used to uncover corporate espionage and insider threats.

A multinational corporation employed OSINT analysts to investigate a series of data breaches and leaks of sensitive company information.

Through OSINT, they traced the leaks back to a disgruntled employee who had been sharing confidential data with competitors.

This discovery allowed the company to take legal action against the employee and strengthen its cybersecurity measures.

OSINT has also been instrumental in tracking the activities of extremist groups and countering radicalization efforts.

Government agencies and counterterrorism units have used OSINT to monitor online platforms, identify recruitment efforts, and track the movements of individuals associated with extremist organizations.

By proactively addressing these threats, they have contributed to national security and public safety.

In the world of journalism, OSINT has become a powerful tool for investigative reporters.

Journalists have used open-source intelligence to uncover corruption, expose human rights abuses, and shed light on government misconduct.

By analyzing publicly available data, conducting online research, and collaborating with OSINT experts, journalists have played a crucial role in holding those in power accountable.

OSINT has also been employed in geopolitical analysis and international relations.

Governments and think tanks use OSINT to monitor global events, track military activities, and assess the intentions of foreign actors.

By analyzing satellite imagery, open-source reports, and social media activity, analysts can provide policymakers with valuable insights for informed decision-making.

In the field of competitive intelligence, businesses use OSINT to gain a competitive edge.

Companies employ OSINT analysts to monitor their competitors, analyze market trends, and gather information on industry developments.

This information helps businesses make strategic decisions, identify emerging opportunities, and stay ahead of their rivals.

Moreover, OSINT has been crucial in the field of threat intelligence.

Cybersecurity firms, in particular, rely on open-source intelligence to detect and respond to emerging cyber threats.

By monitoring underground forums, analyzing malware campaigns, and tracking threat actors, these firms can provide timely warnings and protective measures to their clients.

One notable OSINT success story involves the tracking of a notorious cybercriminal group responsible for a series of high-profile attacks.

By continuously monitoring the group's online activities and analyzing its tactics, OSINT practitioners were able to identify key individuals and provide law enforcement agencies with actionable intelligence.

This collaboration ultimately led to the arrest and dismantling of the criminal organization.

In the realm of political analysis, OSINT has been pivotal in assessing election interference and foreign influence campaigns.

Government agencies and independent researchers use OSINT to identify disinformation campaigns, track online propaganda efforts, and analyze the impact of information warfare.

By scrutinizing social media trends, tracking the spread of fake news, and monitoring online discussions, analysts can provide insights into the manipulation of public opinion.

OSINT success stories demonstrate the versatility and effectiveness of open-source intelligence across a wide range of domains.

These stories highlight the role of OSINT in solving crimes, enhancing cybersecurity, supporting humanitarian efforts, countering extremism, enabling investigative journalism, informing policymaking, and boosting business competitiveness.

The real-world impact of OSINT is evident in its contribution to national security, public safety, corporate strategy, and the pursuit of truth and justice.

These success stories serve as a testament to the value of open-source intelligence in an increasingly interconnected and information-driven world.

Challenges and ethical considerations in OSINT operations are integral aspects of conducting responsible and effective open-source intelligence activities.

One of the primary challenges in OSINT is the sheer volume of available information.

The internet is a vast repository of data, and sifting through this vast sea of information to find relevant and reliable data can be a daunting task.

OSINT practitioners often encounter information overload, which can lead to time-consuming and resource-intensive investigations.

Moreover, the dynamic nature of online information presents a challenge in maintaining the accuracy and timeliness of OSINT data.

Information can change rapidly, and what is true one day may not be accurate the next.

OSINT analysts must constantly verify and update their findings to ensure their relevance and reliability.

Additionally, the credibility of online sources is a persistent challenge in OSINT.

The internet is rife with misinformation, disinformation, and unreliable sources.

OSINT practitioners must critically assess the trustworthiness of the sources they rely on and be vigilant against falling victim to hoaxes or false information.

The lack of standardization in online data poses another challenge in OSINT.

Data may be presented in various formats, languages, and structures, making it challenging to consolidate and analyze information consistently.

OSINT analysts often need to adapt to diverse data sources and formats, which can hinder the efficiency of their operations.

Maintaining operational security, or OPSEC, is a critical concern in OSINT operations.

Analysts must protect their identities and affiliations while conducting investigations, particularly when dealing with sensitive or adversarial subjects.

Failure to maintain OPSEC can jeopardize the safety of the analyst and compromise the integrity of the investigation.

Ethical considerations are paramount in OSINT operations.

One of the core ethical principles in OSINT is respecting individuals' privacy and data protection rights.

OSINT practitioners must avoid intruding into private or protected information without proper authorization or legal justification.

Furthermore, OSINT practitioners should exercise discretion and sensitivity when handling sensitive or personal information.

The publication or dissemination of sensitive data, such as personal addresses or financial information, can have severe consequences and should be avoided.

In addition to privacy concerns, OSINT analysts must navigate legal and regulatory frameworks governing their activities.

Laws regarding data privacy, intellectual property rights, and surveillance can vary widely between countries and regions.

OSINT practitioners must be aware of and compliant with these legal requirements to avoid legal repercussions.

The ethical consideration of attribution is also significant in OSINT.

Attribution involves the identification of the source of information or the origin of online activities.

OSINT analysts must be cautious when attributing actions or statements to specific individuals or entities, as misattribution can harm innocent parties and damage their reputation.

Moreover, OSINT practitioners should exercise restraint in their reporting and avoid making unfounded accusations.

Anonymity is another ethical consideration in OSINT.

While anonymity can protect OSINT practitioners from potential risks, it can also be used for malicious purposes, such as cyberbullying or harassment.

OSINT practitioners must use anonymity responsibly and avoid engaging in unethical or harmful activities.

The potential for unintentional harm is a constant ethical concern in OSINT.

Even well-intentioned investigations can have unintended consequences, such as exposing vulnerable individuals or compromising their safety.

OSINT analysts must carefully weigh the potential benefits of their investigations against the risks of harm and take measures to minimize any negative impact.

Another ethical dilemma in OSINT involves the use of deception.

Some OSINT techniques may require the creation of fake online personas or the use of subterfuge to gather information.

OSINT practitioners should only resort to such tactics when absolutely necessary and with full awareness of the ethical implications.

Transparency and honesty are critical in reporting and disclosure.

OSINT practitioners should be transparent about their methods, sources, and limitations in their findings and reports.

They should also give proper credit to the sources of information they rely on and avoid plagiarism or misrepresentation.

Finally, the ethical responsibility of OSINT practitioners extends to their duty to report illegal or harmful activities they encounter during their investigations.

If OSINT analysts come across evidence of criminal behavior or activities that pose a threat to public safety, they should report this information to the appropriate authorities.

In summary, challenges and ethical considerations are inherent in OSINT operations and must be addressed with diligence and responsibility.

OSINT practitioners must grapple with information overload, source credibility, data standardization, and operational security while adhering to ethical principles.

Respecting privacy, complying with legal frameworks, and minimizing harm are essential aspects of conducting ethical OSINT investigations.

By navigating these challenges and upholding ethical standards, OSINT practitioners can ensure the responsible and effective use of open-source intelligence for various purposes.

BOOK 3
OSINT COMMANDO UNLEASHED
TAKING YOUR SKILLS FROM ENTRY-LEVEL TO ELITE

ROB BOTWRIGHT

Chapter 1: The Journey Begins: Exploring the OSINT Landscape

Embracing the world of open-source intelligence (OSINT) is a journey into the ever-expanding realm of publicly available information.

In an age where data is ubiquitous, accessible, and constantly evolving, OSINT provides a powerful set of tools and techniques to harness this wealth of information for various purposes.

OSINT is not limited to a single domain or discipline; it spans across industries, professions, and interests.

Whether you are a cybersecurity analyst, investigative journalist, business strategist, or simply a curious individual, OSINT can empower you with valuable insights and knowledge.

At its core, OSINT is about leveraging publicly accessible data from a wide range of sources to gain a better understanding of the world around us.

This data can include information from social media, websites, government records, academic publications, news articles, and much more.

The beauty of OSINT lies in its democratizing nature; it levels the playing field by providing access to information that was once the exclusive domain of governments and institutions.

With the right skills and tools, anyone can become an OSINT practitioner and embark on a journey of discovery.

The first step in embracing OSINT is to recognize its potential and significance.

In a world where information is power, OSINT offers a means to unlock that power and use it to your advantage.

Whether you are conducting research, enhancing cybersecurity, tracking global events, or uncovering hidden truths, OSINT can be your ally in the pursuit of knowledge and insight.

One of the fundamental principles of OSINT is the concept of open-source data.

Open-source data refers to information that is publicly available, either by design or inadvertently, without the need for special access or authorization.

This data can be found in countless places, from social media platforms like Twitter and Facebook to government websites, corporate filings, and online forums.

By tapping into these sources, OSINT practitioners can gather a wealth of information on a wide range of topics.

However, it's essential to approach OSINT with a sense of responsibility and ethics.

As you navigate the world of open-source intelligence, you will encounter a vast sea of data, some of which may be sensitive, personal, or protected by privacy laws.

Respecting individuals' privacy rights and complying with legal and ethical standards is paramount in OSINT operations.

Understanding the ethical boundaries and legal frameworks that govern OSINT is a crucial aspect of embracing this field.

Ethics and legality are not mere formalities; they are the foundation upon which responsible OSINT operations are built.

Another key facet of OSINT is the importance of critical thinking and analysis.

As you gather and process information from various sources, it's essential to assess the credibility and reliability of the data.

Not all information is created equal, and discerning fact from fiction is a skill that every OSINT practitioner must hone.

Critical thinking also involves asking questions, verifying sources, and cross-referencing information to ensure accuracy.

In an era of misinformation and disinformation, these skills are more valuable than ever.

One of the remarkable aspects of OSINT is its adaptability.

The tools and techniques used in OSINT are constantly evolving to keep pace with changes in technology and the online landscape.

Embracing OSINT means embracing a continuous learning journey, where you stay updated on the latest tools, methodologies, and best practices.

Whether you are learning about web scraping, geospatial analysis, social media monitoring, or data visualization, there is always something new to explore in the world of OSINT.

Furthermore, OSINT is not a solitary endeavor; it thrives on collaboration and knowledge sharing.

Online communities, forums, and organizations dedicated to OSINT provide platforms for practitioners to exchange ideas, share insights, and learn from one another.

Embracing OSINT means becoming part of this global network of information enthusiasts and contributing your expertise to the collective knowledge base.

As you dive deeper into the world of OSINT, you'll discover its vast applications across various domains.

For cybersecurity professionals, OSINT is a crucial tool in threat detection, vulnerability assessment, and incident response.

It allows them to monitor for potential threats, gather intelligence on adversaries, and proactively protect their systems and data.

Journalists and investigative reporters rely on OSINT to uncover stories, validate sources, and verify facts.

In an era of fast-paced news cycles and digital information, OSINT can be a beacon of truth and transparency.

Businesses and corporate strategists use OSINT to analyze market trends, track competitors, and make informed decisions.

By harnessing the power of publicly available data, they can gain a competitive edge and adapt to changing market dynamics.

Human rights advocates and researchers leverage OSINT to shed light on injustices, document human rights abuses, and advocate for positive change.

The ability to gather and present credible evidence is a potent tool in the pursuit of justice and accountability.

Government agencies and law enforcement use OSINT to enhance national security, monitor threats, and support criminal investigations.

OSINT can provide critical insights into emerging threats and help agencies respond effectively.

Embracing the world of open-source intelligence opens doors to endless possibilities.

Whether you are a beginner taking your first steps into OSINT or an experienced practitioner seeking to deepen your skills, the journey is one of continuous growth and exploration.

It is a journey of discovery, where every piece of information uncovered brings you closer to understanding the world, solving problems, and making informed decisions.

Embracing OSINT is not just about acquiring knowledge; it's about using that knowledge to make a positive impact on the world, whether by protecting digital assets, uncovering hidden truths, or advocating for change.

As you embark on this journey, remember that the world of open-source intelligence is vast and ever-changing, but with the right mindset, ethics, and dedication, you can navigate it successfully and reap its rewards.

The evolution of OSINT techniques is a testament to the adaptability and innovation within the field of open-source intelligence.

From its humble beginnings to its current state, OSINT has continually evolved to meet the challenges and opportunities presented by the digital age.

In the early days of OSINT, the primary sources of information were traditional media outlets, public records, and libraries.

OSINT practitioners relied on newspapers, magazines, and books to gather information, and research often involved physically visiting libraries and archives.

As technology advanced, the internet emerged as a game-changer in the world of OSINT.

The widespread availability of online information revolutionized the way OSINT was conducted.

With search engines, online databases, and digital archives, OSINT practitioners could access a vast amount of data from the comfort of their own computers.

The advent of social media platforms further expanded the scope of OSINT.

Platforms like Facebook, Twitter, and LinkedIn became rich sources of information, offering insights into individuals' personal lives, interests, and connections.

OSINT analysts learned to navigate these platforms, using techniques such as keyword searches, geolocation, and social network analysis to extract valuable intelligence.

The rise of online forums, blogs, and discussion boards added another layer to OSINT operations.

These platforms provided a wealth of user-generated content and discussions on various topics.

OSINT practitioners began monitoring these spaces to gauge public sentiment, track emerging trends, and identify potential threats.

In the world of cybersecurity, OSINT took on a vital role in threat intelligence.

Security professionals recognized that monitoring online sources could yield valuable information about cyber threats and vulnerabilities.

OSINT became an integral part of proactive defense, enabling organizations to stay ahead of cyber adversaries.

The field of OSINT also saw the development of specialized tools and software.

Web scraping tools allowed analysts to automate the collection of data from websites, making it faster and more efficient to gather information.

Geospatial analysis tools enabled the mapping of data to geographical locations, enhancing the understanding of spatial relationships.

Data visualization tools allowed OSINT practitioners to transform raw data into meaningful visual representations, aiding in analysis and decision-making.

The emergence of data mining and machine learning further enhanced the capabilities of OSINT.

These technologies enabled analysts to process large datasets, identify patterns, and extract valuable insights more efficiently.

Machine learning algorithms could be trained to recognize specific information or anomalies in vast amounts of unstructured data.

As OSINT techniques evolved, so did the ethical considerations surrounding the field.

The responsible use of OSINT became a focal point, with practitioners emphasizing privacy, data protection, and compliance with legal and ethical standards.

Ethical OSINT practices involved respecting individuals' privacy rights, verifying information sources, and avoiding the dissemination of false or sensitive data.

Furthermore, the importance of critical thinking and skepticism grew as misinformation and disinformation proliferated online.

OSINT practitioners needed to develop the skills to discern credible sources from unreliable ones and to question the authenticity of online content.

In recent years, OSINT has played a significant role in countering disinformation campaigns and uncovering the truth in an era of fake news.

The field of OSINT continued to expand its horizons beyond the digital realm.

Geospatial intelligence (GEOINT) and social media intelligence (SOCMINT) became integral components of OSINT operations.

GEOINT involved the analysis of geospatial data, such as satellite imagery and location-based information, to gain insights into physical environments and activities.

SOCMINT focused on extracting intelligence from social media platforms, recognizing that these platforms were hubs of communication and information sharing.

The integration of various intelligence disciplines, including HUMINT (human intelligence) and SIGINT (signals intelligence), became a hallmark of advanced OSINT operations.

OSINT analysts recognized that combining multiple sources of intelligence could provide a more comprehensive and accurate picture of complex situations.

OSINT also found applications in various domains beyond cybersecurity and intelligence.

Businesses began using OSINT for competitive intelligence, market research, and brand monitoring.

Journalists and investigative reporters relied on OSINT to uncover stories, verify sources, and fact-check information.

Humanitarian organizations employed OSINT in disaster response and crisis management, utilizing geospatial data and social media analytics to assess the impact of natural disasters and coordinate relief efforts.

In the field of law enforcement, OSINT became a valuable tool in criminal investigations, aiding in the identification of suspects and the tracking of criminal activities.

As OSINT continued to evolve, it became increasingly evident that its potential was limitless.

The ability to gather, analyze, and interpret open-source information had applications in virtually every aspect of human endeavor.

From national security to business strategy, from journalism to academia, OSINT played a vital role in shaping decisions and understanding the world.

The democratization of information through the internet empowered individuals and organizations to harness the power of OSINT for their benefit.

However, with this power came a responsibility to use OSINT ethically and responsibly.

The evolution of OSINT techniques demonstrated that it was not just a static set of tools and methods but a dynamic and ever-changing field.

As technology continued to advance, OSINT would undoubtedly evolve further, presenting new challenges and opportunities.

For those who embraced the world of open-source intelligence, the journey was ongoing, with endless possibilities awaiting discovery in the ever-expanding landscape of publicly available information.

Chapter 2: Building a Strong OSINT Foundation

Understanding core OSINT principles is essential for anyone seeking to navigate the complex world of open-source intelligence effectively.

OSINT, or open-source intelligence, is the process of collecting and analyzing publicly available information from a wide range of sources to gain valuable insights and knowledge.

At its core, OSINT is built on the foundation of open-source data, which includes information that is publicly accessible without the need for special access or authorization.

Open-source data can be found on the internet, in public records, academic publications, social media platforms, and other publicly available sources.

One of the fundamental principles of OSINT is that it is based on information that is legally and ethically obtainable.

OSINT practitioners must adhere to ethical standards and legal guidelines when conducting their investigations.

Respecting individuals' privacy rights and following data protection laws is paramount in OSINT operations.

Another core principle of OSINT is the concept of "need to know."

OSINT analysts should gather and use only the information that is relevant to their specific objectives and within the boundaries of their ethical and legal responsibilities.

The principle of relevance ensures that OSINT operations remain focused and do not infringe on individuals' privacy unnecessarily.

Accuracy is a critical principle in OSINT.

The information gathered must be as accurate as possible to avoid making incorrect conclusions or decisions based on flawed data.

OSINT practitioners should verify the credibility of their sources and cross-reference information when possible to ensure its accuracy.

OSINT operations should also be conducted with transparency and honesty.

This means that OSINT analysts should be open about their methods, sources, and limitations when presenting their findings.

Being transparent helps build trust and credibility in the field of open-source intelligence.

Objectivity is another essential principle in OSINT.

Analysts should strive to remain impartial and free from bias when conducting their investigations and analyzing data.

Objectivity ensures that the results of OSINT operations are based on facts rather than preconceived notions or personal beliefs.

The principle of confidentiality is crucial in OSINT, especially when it comes to protecting sensitive information.

OSINT analysts must handle confidential data responsibly and ensure that it is not disclosed to unauthorized parties.

Maintaining the confidentiality of sources is also vital to protect those who provide information to OSINT practitioners.

Another core principle of OSINT is the continuous improvement of skills and techniques.

The field of open-source intelligence is dynamic, with new tools and methods constantly emerging.

OSINT practitioners should stay updated on the latest developments in the field and be willing to adapt and learn to remain effective.

Collaboration is encouraged in OSINT operations.

Working together with other analysts or experts in related fields can lead to more comprehensive and accurate results. Sharing knowledge and insights within the OSINT community benefits everyone involved.

One of the overarching principles of OSINT is to use the information gathered for lawful and ethical purposes.

OSINT should never be used for illegal or malicious activities, such as hacking, stalking, or harassment.

Respecting the law and ethical standards ensures that OSINT remains a legitimate and responsible field.

The principle of accountability holds OSINT practitioners responsible for their actions and decisions.

If mistakes or errors occur during an investigation, OSINT analysts should take responsibility and make efforts to correct them.

Accountability helps maintain the integrity of the OSINT field.

Flexibility is an essential principle in OSINT.

Analysts should be adaptable and willing to adjust their strategies and techniques based on the evolving landscape of open-source data.

Flexibility allows OSINT practitioners to stay effective and relevant in a rapidly changing environment.

In summary, understanding the core principles of OSINT is fundamental to conducting responsible and effective open-source intelligence operations.

These principles guide the ethical and legal aspects of OSINT, ensuring that information is gathered and used responsibly and ethically.

By adhering to these principles, OSINT practitioners can contribute to the field's integrity and legitimacy while providing valuable insights and knowledge from publicly available sources.

Developing effective research skills is a crucial aspect of mastering the art of open-source intelligence (OSINT).

OSINT relies heavily on the ability to gather, analyze, and interpret vast amounts of publicly available information.

Whether you are a beginner or an experienced OSINT practitioner, honing your research skills is essential to your success in this field.

Effective research begins with setting clear objectives and defining what you aim to achieve through your investigation.

Before you start, you should have a clear understanding of the questions you want to answer or the information you seek.

This initial step helps you stay focused and ensures that your research efforts are purposeful.

Once you have established your objectives, the next step is to determine the sources of information that are most relevant to your investigation.

OSINT offers a wide array of potential sources, including websites, social media platforms, public records, news articles, academic publications, and more.

Identifying the right sources is critical to saving time and energy while obtaining accurate and valuable data.

An important aspect of effective research is conducting systematic searches.

This involves using specific keywords, search operators, and filters to narrow down your search results and find information that is pertinent to your objectives.

Understanding how search engines work and becoming proficient in using advanced search techniques can significantly improve the efficiency of your research.

In addition to traditional search engines like Google, OSINT practitioners often use specialized search engines and tools designed for OSINT purposes.

These tools can help you access data from a wide range of sources, including deep web and dark web content.

As you conduct your research, it's important to keep meticulous records of your findings.

Documenting your sources, the dates of your searches, and the information you uncover ensures that your research is transparent, reproducible, and credible.

Creating a structured system for note-taking and data organization is essential for managing the wealth of information you may encounter.

An often overlooked but crucial aspect of effective research is the ability to critically evaluate the information you find.

Not all sources are equally reliable, and not all information is accurate.

OSINT practitioners must develop a discerning eye for assessing the credibility and relevance of the data they encounter.

Factors to consider when evaluating information include the source's reputation, the date of publication, the presence of corroborating evidence, and any potential biases.

It's important to be skeptical and avoid accepting information at face value.

Cross-referencing information with multiple sources can help confirm its accuracy and reduce the risk of relying on misinformation.

In the field of OSINT, speed can be a critical factor.

Information can become outdated or lose its relevance quickly.

To ensure the timeliness of your research, you must develop efficient workflows and techniques for quickly gathering and analyzing data.

Automation tools and scripts can be valuable in expediting repetitive tasks, such as data collection or data scraping.

However, automation should be used judiciously and in compliance with ethical and legal standards.

Collaboration is another essential element of effective OSINT research.

Working with others who have complementary skills and expertise can lead to more comprehensive and accurate results.

Sharing knowledge, insights, and best practices within the OSINT community can also enhance your research capabilities.

Additionally, networking with experts in related fields can provide access to specialized resources and information sources.

As you progress in your OSINT journey, it's essential to continue learning and staying updated on the latest developments in research techniques and tools.

The field of open-source intelligence is dynamic, and new technologies and methods emerge regularly.

Investing in ongoing education and professional development can help you remain at the forefront of OSINT practices.

Ethical considerations are paramount in OSINT research.

Respecting individuals' privacy rights and adhering to data protection laws is non-negotiable.

You should always obtain information through lawful and ethical means, avoiding any activities that could infringe on privacy or violate legal standards.

OSINT practitioners must also be mindful of the potential consequences of their research.

The information you uncover may have real-world implications, and its use should align with ethical principles and societal norms.

Transparency is essential when sharing OSINT findings with others, whether in an organizational context or for public dissemination.

Clearly presenting your research methods, sources, and limitations ensures that your results can be evaluated and understood by others.

Finally, effective research in OSINT requires adaptability and resilience.

Not all research efforts will yield the desired results, and challenges may arise during investigations.

Being flexible and willing to adjust your approach or pivot when necessary can be a valuable skill in overcoming obstacles.

In summary, developing effective research skills is a fundamental aspect of succeeding in the field of open-source intelligence.

OSINT practitioners must set clear objectives, identify relevant sources, conduct systematic searches, document their findings, critically evaluate information, and prioritize ethical considerations.

Efficiency, collaboration, continuous learning, and adaptability are also crucial components of effective OSINT research.

By honing these skills and adhering to ethical standards, you can enhance your ability to gather and analyze publicly available information effectively, contributing to the field's integrity and the responsible use of OSINT in various domains.

Chapter 3: Spokeo: From Entry-Level Exploration to Elite Mastery

Spokeo is a powerful and versatile online platform that plays a significant role in the world of open-source intelligence (OSINT).

It serves as a comprehensive tool for gathering and analyzing publicly available information, making it a valuable asset for OSINT practitioners.

Next, we will introduce you to Spokeo and its capabilities, providing you with a foundational understanding of how to leverage this tool effectively.

Spokeo is an OSINT tool that specializes in aggregating data from a wide range of sources to create comprehensive profiles of individuals, businesses, and organizations.

It compiles information from public records, social media platforms, online directories, and other publicly accessible sources, providing users with a wealth of data to aid their investigations.

One of Spokeo's key strengths lies in its ability to simplify the process of gathering data from multiple sources and presenting it in an organized and accessible manner.

This streamlines the research process, saving time and effort for OSINT analysts.

Spokeo's user-friendly interface makes it accessible to both beginners and experienced OSINT practitioners.

Its intuitive design allows users to navigate the platform with ease, ensuring a smooth and efficient user experience.

To get started with Spokeo, users can simply create an account and log in to the platform.

Once logged in, you can begin your OSINT investigations by entering a name, email address, phone number, or any other relevant information in the search bar.

Spokeo's search engine will then retrieve and display a list of potential matches based on the provided information.

Users can choose from various subscription options, each offering different levels of access to Spokeo's features and data.

The subscription tiers range from basic plans to more comprehensive options that provide access to advanced search filters and additional data sources.

The availability of these features may vary depending on your subscription level, so it's essential to choose a plan that aligns with your specific OSINT needs and budget.

Spokeo offers various search filters and parameters that allow users to refine their searches and obtain more precise results.

These filters include location, age, education, family members, social media profiles, and more.

By using these filters strategically, OSINT analysts can narrow down their search results to focus on the most relevant and significant information.

Additionally, Spokeo provides users with the option to explore an individual's social media profiles directly from the platform.

This feature allows OSINT practitioners to access and review an individual's online presence, including their posts, photos, and connections on various social media platforms.

Accessing an individual's social media profiles can provide valuable insights into their interests, affiliations, and activities.

Spokeo's database also includes records from public sources such as court records, property records, and business filings.

This information can be particularly useful for conducting background checks, verifying identities, and uncovering potential legal or financial issues.

OSINT analysts can access detailed reports on individuals, which may include personal information, contact details, educational background, employment history, and more.

These reports provide a comprehensive overview of an individual's public profile, making it easier to gather and organize relevant data for your OSINT investigations.

One of the advantages of using Spokeo is its ability to provide contact information for individuals, including phone numbers and email addresses.

This feature can be valuable for connecting with individuals as part of your OSINT investigations or outreach efforts.

Spokeo also offers reverse phone lookup and email search functionalities, allowing users to identify the owners of specific phone numbers or email addresses.

This capability can be helpful in verifying the authenticity of contacts and identifying potential sources of information.

For OSINT analysts seeking to uncover connections and relationships between individuals, Spokeo offers family and relationship mapping.

This feature displays a visual representation of an individual's family members, associates, and acquaintances, helping users understand an individual's social network.

By identifying key connections, OSINT practitioners can explore potential leads and gather more information about their subjects.

Spokeo provides users with the option to save and organize their search results, creating a convenient way to keep track of collected data and revisit it as needed.

This feature can be particularly valuable when conducting in-depth investigations that span multiple sessions or require ongoing monitoring.

In addition to its individual search capabilities, Spokeo also offers tools for researching businesses and organizations.

Users can access detailed reports on businesses, including contact information, industry details, and key personnel.

This feature is valuable for due diligence, competitive intelligence, and market research.

Spokeo's capabilities extend beyond basic searches, with advanced features that cater to the needs of experienced OSINT analysts.

These features include the ability to search for criminal records, court documents, and bankruptcy filings, providing comprehensive insights into an individual's legal history.

Furthermore, Spokeo offers an API (Application Programming Interface) that allows developers to integrate Spokeo's data into their own applications and workflows.

This API can be customized to suit specific OSINT requirements and enhance the efficiency of data retrieval and analysis.

As OSINT continues to evolve, tools like Spokeo play a crucial role in helping analysts access and make sense of publicly available information.

By harnessing the capabilities of Spokeo and mastering its features, OSINT practitioners can conduct more effective investigations, uncover valuable insights, and contribute to their organizations' or clients' missions.

In the chapters that follow, we will delve deeper into Spokeo's functionalities and explore advanced techniques for leveraging this powerful OSINT tool to its fullest potential.

Mastering Spokeo's advanced features is a crucial step for OSINT analysts who aim to become proficient in using this versatile tool to its full potential.

While Spokeo offers a user-friendly interface for basic searches, its advanced features provide a wealth of options and functionalities that can significantly enhance your OSINT investigations.

Next, we will explore these advanced features and guide you through the process of mastering them.

One of the advanced features of Spokeo is its ability to conduct reverse phone number lookups with precision.

This feature allows you to enter a phone number and retrieve detailed information about the individual or entity associated with that number.

Reverse phone lookups can be invaluable for verifying identities, confirming the authenticity of contacts, and uncovering hidden connections.

Spokeo also offers an email search feature that enables you to search for individuals using their email addresses.

This can be particularly useful for locating specific individuals or verifying the legitimacy of email contacts in your OSINT investigations.

The advanced search filters in Spokeo allow you to refine your queries further.

These filters include options for narrowing down your search results based on criteria such as location, age, education, and more.

By using these filters strategically, you can focus your investigations on the most relevant and significant data.

Spokeo's deep web search capabilities extend beyond what is accessible through traditional search engines.

It can access and retrieve data from sources that may not be easily discoverable through standard online searches.

This feature provides OSINT practitioners with access to a broader spectrum of information, increasing the depth and comprehensiveness of their investigations.

One of the valuable advanced functionalities of Spokeo is its ability to perform comprehensive background checks on individuals.

These background checks can include details such as criminal records, court records, and financial histories.

This information can be critical for due diligence, risk assessment, and uncovering potential legal or financial issues.

Spokeo's family and relationship mapping feature allows you to visualize an individual's connections and relationships.

This advanced feature provides a visual representation of an individual's family members, associates, and acquaintances, helping you understand their social network.

By identifying key connections, you can explore leads and gather more information about your subjects.

Spokeo also offers a feature called "People Also Viewed."

This feature displays a list of individuals who are related or connected in some way to your search subject.

Exploring these related profiles can lead to discovering new sources of information and connections that may be relevant to your investigations.

The ability to save and organize your search results is an advanced feature that can greatly enhance your workflow.

By creating folders and categorizing your findings, you can keep track of collected data, revisit it as needed, and maintain organized records of your OSINT investigations.

Spokeo's API (Application Programming Interface) is a powerful tool for advanced users and developers.

The API allows you to integrate Spokeo's data into your own applications, scripts, or workflows, providing a high degree of customization and control.

Developers can leverage the API to automate data retrieval, perform batch searches, and create tailored solutions that align with specific OSINT requirements.

Furthermore, Spokeo's API offers advanced users the ability to access data programmatically and integrate it seamlessly into their existing OSINT processes.

Advanced users can also benefit from Spokeo's comprehensive data sources.

Spokeo aggregates information from a vast array of publicly available sources, including social media platforms, public records, online directories, and more.

This extensive data coverage ensures that OSINT practitioners have access to a wide range of information to support their investigations.

In summary, mastering Spokeo's advanced features empowers OSINT analysts to conduct more in-depth and effective investigations.

These advanced functionalities, including reverse phone number lookups, email searches, advanced search filters, deep web access, comprehensive background checks, family and relationship mapping, and API integration, provide a powerful toolkit for gathering and analyzing publicly available information.

By becoming proficient in these advanced features, OSINT practitioners can uncover valuable insights, verify identities, and discover hidden connections that may be critical to their investigative objectives.

In the following chapters, we will delve even deeper into Spokeo's capabilities and explore advanced techniques for harnessing its full potential in the realm of open-source intelligence.

Chapter 4: Spiderfoot Unleashed: Advanced Techniques for OSINT Pros

Advanced Spiderfoot modules and customization are essential components of mastering the capabilities of this versatile open-source intelligence (OSINT) tool.

As you progress in your journey to become an OSINT expert, delving into Spiderfoot's advanced features will enable you to conduct more comprehensive and targeted investigations. Next, we will explore the advanced modules and customization options that Spiderfoot offers, providing you with valuable insights and techniques.

Spiderfoot is known for its modular and extensible architecture, allowing users to add custom modules and adapt the tool to their specific OSINT needs.

This flexibility empowers OSINT practitioners to tailor Spiderfoot to their unique requirements and enhance their investigative capabilities.

One of the key aspects of Spiderfoot's advanced functionality is the ability to create custom transforms.

Transforms are scripts that retrieve and process data from external sources.

By developing custom transforms, you can expand Spiderfoot's data collection capabilities beyond its built-in modules.

This customization feature is especially valuable when dealing with specialized data sources or when you need to integrate Spiderfoot with external tools and APIs.

Custom transforms enable OSINT analysts to gather information from websites, databases, or any other online resource that may contain relevant data.

Developing custom transforms requires scripting knowledge, and Spiderfoot supports Python and JavaScript as scripting languages for this purpose.

With custom transforms, you can access data that may not be available through Spiderfoot's default modules, allowing you to uncover valuable insights in your investigations.

Spiderfoot's advanced modules provide additional functionalities that can greatly enhance your OSINT efforts.

These modules offer specialized capabilities, such as geolocation, email analysis, cryptocurrency investigation, and more.

By using these modules strategically, you can target specific aspects of your investigations and gain deeper insights into your subjects.

For example, the geolocation module allows you to determine the physical location of IP addresses, domains, and other network-related information.

This can be valuable for tracking the geographic origins of online activities, identifying potential threats, or confirming the location of a target.

The email analysis module, on the other hand, enables you to analyze email addresses and associated domains, providing information about their reputation, history, and any associated threats.

Email analysis can be crucial for uncovering phishing attempts, verifying the legitimacy of email contacts, and tracing the origins of suspicious communications.

Cryptocurrency investigation is another specialized area covered by Spiderfoot's modules.

With this module, OSINT practitioners can trace cryptocurrency transactions, addresses, and wallet information.

This can be particularly useful when dealing with subjects involved in cryptocurrency-related activities, financial crimes, or online fraud.

The customization options in Spiderfoot extend to the user interface as well.

You can personalize your Spiderfoot instance by configuring settings, creating custom tags for entities, and defining notification preferences.

Customization allows you to streamline your workflow and adapt Spiderfoot to your preferred working style.

By tailoring the tool to your specific needs, you can improve efficiency and focus on the aspects of OSINT that matter most to your investigations.

Spiderfoot also offers the ability to schedule scans and automate data collection.

This advanced feature enables OSINT analysts to set up recurring scans for specific targets, domains, or IP addresses.

Automation saves time and ensures that your investigations remain up-to-date, especially when monitoring subjects over an extended period.

Scheduled scans can be invaluable for tracking changes in online profiles, identifying emerging threats, or conducting ongoing monitoring of individuals or organizations.

Another advanced feature in Spiderfoot is its support for multiple profiles.

This capability allows you to manage different sets of configurations, modules, and transforms for various investigations.

By creating separate profiles, you can maintain organization and efficiency when working on multiple cases simultaneously.

This feature is particularly useful for OSINT professionals who handle a diverse range of investigations and need to keep their work separate and organized.

When it comes to customizing Spiderfoot, understanding its data sources is crucial.

Spiderfoot leverages various data sources, such as public APIs, web scraping, WHOIS information, DNS records, and more.

By comprehending the strengths and limitations of these data sources, you can make informed decisions when customizing your Spiderfoot instance and selecting the most appropriate modules and transforms for your investigations.

Additionally, Spiderfoot offers integration with other OSINT tools and platforms.

You can connect Spiderfoot to external data sources, import data from other tools, or export your findings to external systems for further analysis or reporting.

Integration capabilities expand the reach and impact of your OSINT investigations, allowing you to leverage a wider ecosystem of tools and resources.

Customization and advanced modules in Spiderfoot empower OSINT practitioners to tailor their investigations to their specific needs and objectives.

By creating custom transforms, utilizing advanced modules, and personalizing the tool's settings, you can gather deeper insights, automate data collection, and streamline your workflow.

Furthermore, Spiderfoot's support for multiple profiles, automation, and integration enhances your efficiency and flexibility in conducting OSINT investigations.

In the following chapters, we will delve deeper into specific advanced modules and customization techniques, providing practical guidance and examples to help you leverage Spiderfoot's full potential in your OSINT endeavors.

Real-world applications of Spiderfoot encompass a wide

range of scenarios where this powerful open-source intelligence (OSINT) tool proves invaluable.

From cybersecurity and threat analysis to corporate due diligence and law enforcement investigations, Spiderfoot plays a crucial role in gathering and analyzing publicly available information to support decision-making and intelligence gathering.

Next, we will explore some of the practical and real-world applications of Spiderfoot and how it contributes to addressing various challenges.

In the realm of cybersecurity, Spiderfoot is a valuable asset for identifying vulnerabilities and potential threats.

Security professionals use Spiderfoot to conduct reconnaissance on their own networks and systems, helping them uncover weaknesses that malicious actors might exploit.

By scanning for open ports, discovering exposed services, and assessing the security posture of their infrastructure, organizations can proactively address vulnerabilities and enhance their cybersecurity defenses.

Spiderfoot's capability to gather information about domain names, IP addresses, and network-related data aids in identifying potential security risks.

For instance, organizations can use Spiderfoot to track down rogue or unauthorized IP addresses within their networks, ensuring that all network activity is accounted for and secure.

Beyond internal network security, Spiderfoot is also utilized to monitor and investigate external threats.

Security teams can use Spiderfoot to gather information about potential threats from external sources, such as known malicious domains, suspicious IP addresses, or malware indicators.

By continuously monitoring these external factors, organizations can proactively defend against cyberattacks and mitigate potential risks.

In the corporate world, due diligence is a critical process, especially during mergers, acquisitions, partnerships, or investments.

Spiderfoot helps organizations conduct thorough due diligence by providing insights into the background and reputation of potential business partners or targets.

By collecting information about key individuals, organizations, and their online presence, Spiderfoot enables decision-makers to assess the trustworthiness and integrity of the entities involved.

Furthermore, Spiderfoot assists in identifying any undisclosed affiliations or associations that might raise concerns during the due diligence process.

Financial institutions and regulatory agencies also employ Spiderfoot for compliance and fraud detection.

By analyzing data related to individuals or entities, Spiderfoot helps detect suspicious activities, potentially fraudulent transactions, or regulatory violations.

This is particularly valuable in the fight against financial crimes such as money laundering, fraud, and identity theft.

Law enforcement agencies leverage Spiderfoot to aid in their investigations, especially when dealing with cases involving cybercrime, missing persons, or criminal networks.

Spiderfoot's data collection capabilities assist investigators in gathering information about suspects, their online activities, and their digital footprint.

This information can be crucial in identifying leads, establishing connections, and building a case against individuals or groups involved in criminal activities.

In the domain of threat intelligence, Spiderfoot is an essential tool for collecting and analyzing indicators of compromise (IOCs) and other threat-related data.

Cybersecurity professionals and threat analysts use Spiderfoot to track malicious actors, investigate cyberattacks, and identify patterns in cyber threat landscapes.

By correlating data from various sources, Spiderfoot aids in attributing cyber threats and understanding the tactics, techniques, and procedures (TTPs) employed by threat actors.

Non-profit organizations and investigative journalists also utilize Spiderfoot for research and investigative reporting.

Spiderfoot helps uncover hidden connections, expose misinformation campaigns, and shed light on controversial topics by aggregating data from diverse sources.

Its capabilities enable researchers to analyze social media profiles, track the spread of disinformation, and reveal the network of actors involved in spreading false narratives.

Human resources professionals employ Spiderfoot in background checks and vetting processes.

By collecting information about job applicants, candidates, or potential employees, HR teams can verify identities, check qualifications, and assess an individual's online presence.

This helps organizations make informed hiring decisions and ensure that candidates align with their values and requirements.

In the world of competitive intelligence, Spiderfoot supports businesses in gathering information about their competitors, market trends, and industry developments.

By monitoring competitors' online activities, social media presence, and public records, organizations can gain insights into their strategies, strengths, and weaknesses.

This intelligence aids in making informed decisions and staying competitive in the market.

In summary, Spiderfoot's real-world applications span a wide spectrum of industries and use cases.

From cybersecurity and threat intelligence to due diligence, law enforcement, and investigative journalism, Spiderfoot provides valuable insights and data collection capabilities to support decision-making, enhance security, and uncover hidden connections.

Its versatility and flexibility make it a valuable tool for professionals and organizations across various domains, contributing to their success in addressing the challenges they face.

Chapter 5: SEON: Elevating Your Skills to Elite Levels

SEON's advanced features and functionality are the cornerstones of its effectiveness as an open-source intelligence (OSINT) tool.

As you delve deeper into SEON, understanding and mastering these advanced capabilities will empower you to conduct more comprehensive and insightful investigations.

Next, we will explore the advanced features and functionality that SEON offers, providing you with practical insights and techniques to elevate your OSINT skills.

SEON's strength lies in its ability to harness the power of open-source intelligence by aggregating and analyzing data from various online sources.

One of its advanced features is its extensive coverage of web resources, including social media platforms, websites, online databases, and public records.

This breadth of data sources ensures that SEON users have access to a wide range of information to support their investigations.

SEON also offers a powerful search engine that allows users to query specific keywords, names, or entities across multiple online sources simultaneously.

This feature enables OSINT practitioners to efficiently locate information related to their subjects and uncover hidden connections or mentions.

Another advanced capability of SEON is its social media analysis tools.

SEON can scrape and analyze data from social media platforms, providing insights into an individual's online presence, behavior, and network.

This is invaluable for profiling subjects, understanding their interests, and identifying potential leads or associations.

SEON's ability to perform sentiment analysis on social media posts is another noteworthy feature.

Sentiment analysis helps OSINT analysts gauge the emotional tone or sentiment expressed in online content, whether it's positive, negative, or neutral.

This can be particularly useful when monitoring public sentiment about specific topics, individuals, or events.

SEON's geolocation capabilities allow users to track and map the locations associated with subjects or online activities.

By mapping out geographic data, investigators can visualize the physical movements, travel patterns, or affiliations of individuals or entities.

This is vital for understanding the geographic aspects of an investigation and identifying potential points of interest.

SEON also offers advanced link analysis tools that help users uncover connections and relationships between entities.

By analyzing links, mentions, or references in online content, investigators can build visual representations of networks and associations.

This can reveal hidden affiliations, uncover key players in a network, and provide a comprehensive view of the relationships surrounding a subject.

Additionally, SEON supports the extraction and analysis of metadata from various file types, including documents, images, and videos.

Metadata can contain valuable information such as timestamps, authorship details, and location data.

Analyzing metadata can provide insights into the origin and history of digital content, aiding investigators in verifying authenticity and tracing the source of information.

SEON's ability to conduct deep web searches is a distinctive feature that sets it apart.

The deep web comprises internet content that is not indexed by standard search engines.

SEON can access and retrieve data from these hidden sources, providing OSINT practitioners with access to a broader spectrum of information.

This is especially valuable for uncovering information that may not be readily accessible through traditional online searches.

Moreover, SEON offers an API (Application Programming Interface) that allows for integration with other tools and systems.

This advanced functionality enables users to automate data retrieval, conduct batch queries, and streamline their OSINT workflows.

By integrating SEON with their existing tools and processes, OSINT professionals can enhance their efficiency and extend the reach of their investigations.

SEON's reporting and visualization capabilities are another set of advanced features.

Users can generate comprehensive reports that consolidate their findings, analysis, and insights into a coherent document.

These reports can be customized to suit specific reporting requirements and are valuable for sharing the results of an OSINT investigation with stakeholders or colleagues.

Furthermore, SEON's visualization tools allow users to create interactive visual representations of data, such as graphs, charts, and maps.

These visualizations can simplify complex relationships, patterns, or trends, making it easier to convey critical information to others.

In summary, SEON's advanced features and functionality are pivotal in enhancing the capabilities of OSINT analysts and investigators.

From its extensive data coverage, social media analysis, and sentiment analysis to geolocation, link analysis, deep web access, and API integration, SEON provides a comprehensive toolkit for gathering, analyzing, and visualizing open-source intelligence.

By mastering these advanced features, OSINT practitioners can uncover deeper insights, verify information, and map out connections that are essential to their investigative objectives.

In the following chapters, we will delve further into SEON's advanced functionalities, providing practical guidance and real-world examples to help you leverage its full potential in your OSINT endeavors.

Conducting elite-level investigations with SEON requires a deep understanding of its advanced capabilities and the ability to apply them strategically to gather critical intelligence.

As you progress in your open-source intelligence (OSINT) journey, honing your skills with SEON will enable you to tackle complex investigations and extract valuable insights.

Next, we will explore the techniques and methodologies for conducting elite-level investigations using SEON.

To embark on elite-level investigations with SEON, it's essential to begin with a well-defined objective.

Clearly define your investigation's purpose, scope, and the information you aim to gather.

Elite-level investigations often involve high-stakes scenarios, such as cybersecurity incidents, threat intelligence, or criminal cases, where precision and accuracy are paramount.

Next, consider the breadth and depth of your data sources.

SEON offers an extensive range of sources, including social media platforms, websites, databases, and public records.

For elite-level investigations, it's crucial to cast a wide net, ensuring that you collect data from diverse sources to create a comprehensive picture.

Additionally, SEON's advanced search capabilities allow you to query specific keywords, names, or entities across multiple online sources simultaneously.

Take advantage of this feature to pinpoint relevant information efficiently.

In elite-level investigations, time is often a critical factor.

SEON's real-time monitoring capabilities enable you to stay up-to-date with developments related to your investigation.

Configure SEON to monitor specific keywords, subjects, or entities, and receive alerts when new information surfaces.

This proactive approach ensures that you don't miss critical updates or emerging threats.

SEON's geolocation capabilities are invaluable for elite-level investigations.

Use geolocation tools to track and map the physical locations associated with subjects or online activities.

This can provide essential context, especially when dealing with incidents that have a geographic dimension, such as cyberattacks or criminal operations.

In elite-level investigations, analyzing social media activity becomes crucial.

SEON's social media analysis tools enable you to scrape and analyze data from various platforms, including posts, comments, and profiles.

Look for patterns, trends, or anomalies in social media behavior that may reveal insights or connections.

Sentiment analysis can provide further depth to your investigation.

By assessing the emotional tone expressed in online content, you can gauge public sentiment and identify potential sentiment-driven actions or reactions.

Deep web access is a distinctive feature of SEON that should not be overlooked in elite-level investigations.

The deep web contains a wealth of information that is not indexed by standard search engines.

SEON's ability to access and retrieve data from deep web sources can uncover hidden information that may be critical to your investigation.

Anonymity and privacy are common concerns in elite-level investigations.

SEON's capabilities include the ability to uncover hidden online identities, aliases, or pseudonyms used by individuals or groups.

This can help identify actors attempting to conceal their true identities or affiliations.

SEON's link analysis tools are powerful for revealing connections and relationships between entities.

Use these tools to build visual representations of networks, affiliations, or associations.

Link analysis can uncover hidden connections, identify key players, and provide a comprehensive view of the relationships surrounding a subject.

Metadata analysis is another advanced technique that can provide valuable insights.

SEON supports the extraction and analysis of metadata from various file types, including documents, images, and videos.

Metadata can reveal timestamps, authorship details, and location data, helping verify the authenticity and origin of digital content.

Elite-level investigations often involve in-depth research into specific subjects.

SEON's ability to perform deep dives into individuals, organizations, or topics allows you to gather comprehensive information.

Create detailed profiles and timelines to track the history, activities, and affiliations of subjects over time.

SEON's reporting and visualization capabilities play a vital role in elite-level investigations.

Generate comprehensive reports that consolidate your findings, analysis, and insights into a coherent document.

Customize reports to meet specific reporting requirements, ensuring that you can communicate your findings effectively to stakeholders or colleagues.

Visualizations, such as graphs, charts, and maps, can simplify complex relationships, patterns, or trends, making it easier to convey critical information.

Collaboration is often essential in elite-level investigations.

SEON's capabilities for sharing findings, reports, and visualizations with team members or external partners facilitate collaboration and information sharing.

Furthermore, SEON's API (Application Programming Interface) integration allows for seamless connectivity with other tools and systems used in elite-level investigations.

By integrating SEON into your existing workflow, you can enhance efficiency and streamline the investigation process.

In elite-level investigations, ethical considerations and legal compliance are paramount.

Ensure that your investigative practices adhere to ethical guidelines and legal regulations to maintain the integrity of your work.

Elite-level investigations may involve sensitive or confidential information.

Implement robust security measures to protect your data and ensure that your investigative activities remain confidential.

In summary, conducting elite-level investigations with SEON requires a comprehensive approach that leverages its advanced features and functionality.

From defining clear objectives and casting a wide net of data sources to utilizing real-time monitoring, geolocation, social media analysis, and deep web access, SEON empowers OSINT practitioners to tackle complex investigations with precision and efficiency.

By mastering these advanced techniques and adhering to ethical and legal standards, you can achieve success in elite-level investigations and contribute to the field of open-source intelligence.

Chapter 6: Lampyre: Advanced Tools and Techniques for Elite Commandos

Lampyre's advanced data analysis tools are at the forefront of open-source intelligence (OSINT) investigations, providing analysts with the means to extract valuable insights from vast amounts of data.

As you progress in your OSINT journey, understanding and harnessing Lampyre's advanced capabilities will enable you to conduct more thorough and insightful investigations.

Next, we will explore Lampyre's advanced data analysis tools and techniques, providing you with practical insights on how to leverage them effectively.

Lampyre's strength lies in its ability to collect, analyze, and visualize diverse data sources, making it a powerful asset for OSINT professionals.

One of its advanced features is its capability to conduct deep web searches, accessing and retrieving data from sources not indexed by standard search engines.

This provides investigators with access to a wealth of information that may be crucial to their investigations.

Lampyre's data enrichment tools allow users to enrich existing data with additional information from various sources.

This can include adding geolocation data to IP addresses, retrieving social media profiles based on usernames, or extracting metadata from files.

By enhancing data with contextual information, investigators can gain deeper insights into their subjects.

The tool's link analysis capabilities are particularly valuable for understanding connections and relationships between entities.

Lampyre enables users to build visual representations of networks, affiliations, or associations, making it easier to identify key players and hidden connections.

This is essential in complex investigations where uncovering the structure of a network is crucial.

Lampyre also offers advanced data visualization tools that transform complex data into easily digestible visual representations.

Users can create interactive graphs, charts, and maps, facilitating a better understanding of data relationships and patterns.

This aids in conveying critical information to stakeholders and decision-makers.

In addition to traditional data sources, Lampyre has the capability to analyze data from social media platforms.

This is particularly valuable for profiling individuals, tracking online behavior, and identifying potential leads or associations.

Sentiment analysis is another advanced feature of Lampyre.

By assessing the emotional tone expressed in social media posts or content, investigators can gauge public sentiment surrounding specific subjects or events.

This can be essential when monitoring public reactions or assessing potential threats.

Lampyre's geolocation tools enable users to track and map physical locations associated with online activities.

This is especially useful in investigations where geographic context plays a significant role, such as cyberattacks or criminal operations.

Metadata analysis is a critical tool for verifying the authenticity and origin of digital content.

Lampyre supports the extraction and analysis of metadata from various file types, providing valuable insights into timestamps, authorship details, and location data.

This helps investigators confirm the legitimacy of digital content and trace its source.

Advanced data analysis often involves deep dives into specific subjects.

Lampyre enables users to create detailed profiles and timelines, tracking the history, activities, and affiliations of subjects over time.

This comprehensive view is crucial in understanding the context and background of individuals or entities.

Lampyre's data export and reporting capabilities allow users to create comprehensive reports that consolidate their findings, analysis, and insights into a coherent document.

These reports can be customized to meet specific reporting requirements and are invaluable for sharing results with stakeholders or colleagues.

Collaboration is essential in advanced OSINT investigations.

Lampyre supports sharing findings, reports, and visualizations with team members or external partners, facilitating effective collaboration and information sharing.

Furthermore, Lampyre's API (Application Programming Interface) integration capabilities enable users to connect with other tools and systems used in their investigative workflows.

By seamlessly integrating Lampyre into their existing processes, OSINT professionals can enhance efficiency and streamline their investigations.

Ethical considerations and legal compliance are paramount in advanced OSINT investigations.

Ensure that your investigative practices adhere to ethical guidelines and legal regulations to maintain the integrity of your work.

Additionally, elite-level investigations may involve sensitive or confidential information.

Implement robust security measures to protect your data and ensure the confidentiality of your investigative activities. In summary, Lampyre's advanced data analysis tools are indispensable for OSINT professionals conducting in-depth investigations.

From deep web access, data enrichment, and link analysis to data visualization, sentiment analysis, and geolocation tools, Lampyre provides a comprehensive toolkit for gathering, analyzing, and visualizing open-source intelligence.

By mastering these advanced techniques and adhering to ethical and legal standards, you can achieve success in advanced OSINT investigations and contribute significantly to the field of open-source intelligence.

Uncovering hidden insights with Lampyre is a crucial aspect of open-source intelligence (OSINT) investigations, allowing analysts to reveal concealed information and patterns within vast datasets.

As you advance in your OSINT journey, understanding how to effectively use Lampyre's capabilities for uncovering hidden insights will significantly enhance your investigative skills.

Next, we will explore Lampyre's tools and techniques for uncovering hidden insights and provide practical guidance on how to apply them.

Lampyre's strength lies in its ability to collect, analyze, and visualize diverse data sources, making it a powerful asset for OSINT professionals.

One of its key features is the capacity to conduct deep web searches, accessing and retrieving data from sources not indexed by standard search engines.

This provides investigators with access to a wealth of information that may be concealed from typical online searches.

Data enrichment is another powerful feature of Lampyre. It enables users to enhance their existing datasets with additional information from various sources, such as adding geolocation data to IP addresses or extracting metadata from files. By enriching data, investigators can uncover hidden insights and gain a deeper understanding of their subjects.

Lampyre's link analysis capabilities are invaluable for uncovering connections and relationships between entities. By visually mapping out networks, affiliations, or associations, users can identify hidden connections and key players within a network.

This is particularly essential in complex investigations where understanding the structure of a network is critical. Lampyre also offers advanced data visualization tools, allowing users to transform complex data into easily digestible visual representations.

Interactive graphs, charts, and maps help investigators identify patterns, relationships, and anomalies within their data, leading to the discovery of hidden insights.

In addition to traditional data sources, Lampyre can analyze data from social media platforms, which can be a goldmine of hidden insights.

Profiling individuals, tracking online behavior, and identifying potential leads or associations are all possible through social media analysis.

Sentiment analysis is another powerful tool that can uncover hidden insights within social media content.

By evaluating the emotional tone expressed in posts or content, investigators can gain insight into public sentiment surrounding specific subjects or events, revealing hidden sentiments and reactions.

Geolocation tools are essential for uncovering hidden insights related to physical locations associated with online activities.

This is especially valuable in investigations where geographic context plays a significant role, such as cyberattacks or criminal operations with hidden locations.

Metadata analysis is a critical technique for verifying the authenticity and origin of digital content.

Lampyre supports the extraction and analysis of metadata from various file types, providing insights into timestamps, authorship details, and location data.

This helps investigators confirm the legitimacy of digital content and uncover hidden information embedded within metadata.

In-depth research into specific subjects often requires detailed profiles and timelines.

Lampyre's capabilities enable users to create comprehensive profiles, tracking the history, activities, and affiliations of subjects over time.

This comprehensive view can reveal hidden insights and context that may not be immediately apparent.

Data export and reporting are vital for consolidating findings and communicating insights effectively.

Lampyre's data export and reporting capabilities allow users to create comprehensive reports tailored to specific requirements.

These reports are instrumental in sharing hidden insights with stakeholders or colleagues, ensuring that the information is effectively conveyed.

Collaboration is often essential in OSINT investigations, and Lampyre supports this by allowing findings, reports, and visualizations to be shared with team members or external partners.

This facilitates effective collaboration and the sharing of hidden insights with others involved in the investigation.

Lampyre's API (Application Programming Interface) integration capabilities provide further flexibility.

Users can seamlessly integrate Lampyre into their existing workflows and connect with other tools and systems used in their investigations.

This streamlines the investigative process and enhances efficiency when uncovering hidden insights.

Ethical considerations and legal compliance are paramount when uncovering hidden insights in OSINT investigations.

Maintaining ethical standards and complying with legal regulations is crucial to the integrity of your work.

Additionally, ensuring the security and confidentiality of sensitive or confidential information is vital when uncovering hidden insights in elite-level investigations.

In summary, Lampyre's tools and techniques for uncovering hidden insights are indispensable for OSINT professionals seeking to extract valuable information and patterns from extensive datasets.

From deep web access and data enrichment to link analysis, data visualization, and sentiment analysis, Lampyre provides a comprehensive toolkit for discovering hidden insights within open-source intelligence.

By mastering these techniques and adhering to ethical and legal standards, you can successfully uncover hidden insights and contribute significantly to the field of open-source intelligence.

Chapter 7: Data Analysis and Visualization for Elite OSINT Professionals

Advanced data analysis methods and tools are the cornerstone of effective decision-making and insights extraction in the modern world of information overload.

As data continues to grow exponentially, the need for advanced techniques to analyze and derive meaning from it becomes increasingly important.

Next, we will explore advanced data analysis methods and the tools that facilitate these techniques, providing you with a deeper understanding of how to extract valuable insights from complex datasets.

Data analysis is the process of inspecting, cleaning, transforming, and modeling data to discover useful information, inform conclusions, and support decision-making.

Advanced data analysis methods go beyond basic statistical techniques and delve into more complex and sophisticated approaches to uncover patterns, trends, and hidden insights.

One of the fundamental aspects of advanced data analysis is the utilization of machine learning algorithms.

Machine learning is a subset of artificial intelligence that enables computers to learn and make predictions or decisions without being explicitly programmed.

These algorithms can be applied to vast datasets to identify patterns or make predictions, greatly enhancing the depth of analysis.

Clustering is an advanced data analysis method that involves grouping similar data points together.

This can reveal hidden structures or associations within the data, making it easier to understand complex relationships.

Principal Component Analysis (PCA) is another powerful technique used in advanced data analysis.

PCA reduces the dimensionality of data while preserving important information, making it easier to visualize and analyze complex datasets.

Time series analysis is crucial when dealing with data that changes over time, such as stock prices, weather patterns, or sales data.

Advanced time series techniques can uncover trends, seasonality, and anomalies in the data, providing valuable insights for decision-making.

Natural Language Processing (NLP) is an advanced data analysis method that focuses on analyzing and interpreting human language data.

This is particularly useful for analyzing text data, social media content, or customer reviews, allowing organizations to gain insights from unstructured text.

Advanced data analysis tools play a pivotal role in implementing these methods effectively.

Data visualization tools are essential for representing complex data in a visual format, making it easier to interpret and derive insights.

Tools like Tableau, Power BI, or Python libraries like Matplotlib and Seaborn enable users to create interactive charts, graphs, and dashboards.

Advanced statistical software packages, such as R or Python with libraries like SciPy and Statsmodels, provide the necessary tools to perform advanced statistical analyses.

These packages offer a wide range of statistical tests and models, allowing users to explore relationships and make informed decisions based on data.

Machine learning libraries, like TensorFlow, PyTorch, or scikit-learn in Python, empower users to implement sophisticated machine learning algorithms.

These libraries provide pre-built algorithms and tools for training, testing, and deploying machine learning models on diverse datasets.

Data preprocessing tools, such as Pandas in Python, are crucial for cleaning, transforming, and organizing data before analysis.

These tools enable users to handle missing data, standardize variables, and prepare data for advanced analysis methods.

Text analysis libraries like NLTK (Natural Language Toolkit) or spaCy are essential for advanced text analysis and NLP tasks.

These libraries provide tools for tokenization, sentiment analysis, entity recognition, and more, making it easier to extract insights from text data.

Time series analysis packages like Statsmodels or Prophet are specialized tools for in-depth time series analysis.

They offer a range of techniques, from decomposition and forecasting to anomaly detection in time-based data.

Advanced data analysis often involves combining multiple data sources to gain a holistic view.

Data integration tools like Apache Nifi or Talend simplify the process of extracting, transforming, and loading (ETL) data from various sources into a unified dataset.

Data mining tools like RapidMiner or Weka are designed for discovering patterns and relationships in large datasets.

They can uncover hidden insights, such as market trends, customer behavior, or fraud detection, by applying machine learning algorithms to the data.

Big data processing frameworks like Hadoop and Apache Spark are essential for analyzing large-scale datasets that exceed the capabilities of traditional databases.

These frameworks enable distributed processing and storage of data, allowing for advanced analytics on massive datasets.

Simulation software like Monte Carlo simulation tools is used to model and analyze complex systems or processes.

These tools help in understanding the impact of various parameters on outcomes and making informed decisions.

In summary, advanced data analysis methods and tools are indispensable for gaining deeper insights and making informed decisions in today's data-driven world.

Machine learning algorithms, clustering, PCA, time series analysis, and NLP techniques expand the analytical toolkit, enabling users to uncover hidden patterns and relationships within complex datasets.

Coupled with advanced data analysis tools like data visualization, statistical software, machine learning libraries, and data integration tools, these methods empower analysts to extract valuable insights from diverse and vast datasets.

By mastering these advanced data analysis techniques and using the right tools, organizations and individuals can make more informed decisions, improve processes, and gain a competitive edge in various fields.

Visualizing OSINT data is a critical step in transforming raw information into actionable intelligence.

Effective visualization techniques enable analysts, investigators, and decision-makers to understand complex datasets, identify patterns, and make informed choices based on the insights derived.

Next, we will explore the importance of visualizing OSINT data and various visualization methods that facilitate the extraction of actionable intelligence.

Visualizing data is the process of representing information graphically, making it easier to comprehend, analyze, and interpret.

OSINT data can be vast, diverse, and dynamic, making visualization an essential tool for gaining actionable intelligence.

One of the primary goals of visualizing OSINT data is to simplify complex information, making it more accessible to a wider audience, including those without a technical background.

Visualization aids in storytelling, allowing analysts to convey their findings effectively and enabling decision-makers to grasp the significance of the information presented.

Charts, graphs, and diagrams are common types of visualizations used in OSINT.

Bar charts are suitable for comparing values between different categories, while line charts help track changes in data over time, providing insights into trends and patterns.

Pie charts are useful for displaying proportions and percentages within a whole, helping to highlight significant components.

Scatter plots reveal relationships between two variables, making it possible to identify correlations or anomalies.

Heatmaps are effective for displaying data density, making it easier to spot concentrations or gaps in the data.

Maps, including geographic information system (GIS) visualizations, are powerful tools for displaying location-based data.

Geospatial visualizations enable analysts to map out events, trends, or patterns on a geographical scale, helping to identify actionable intelligence related to specific locations.

Network diagrams are valuable when visualizing relationships and connections between entities.

They are particularly useful in OSINT investigations involving individuals, organizations, or cyber threats, where understanding the network structure is essential for actionable intelligence.

Sankey diagrams illustrate the flow of data or resources between different stages or components, aiding in the identification of bottlenecks or inefficiencies in processes.

Word clouds are helpful for visualizing text data, highlighting frequently occurring words or phrases, which can provide insights into common themes or topics.

Time series visualizations, such as Gantt charts or calendar heatmaps, are essential when analyzing temporal data.

They help identify patterns, anomalies, or trends over time, contributing to actionable intelligence in various domains, including finance, security, and marketing.

Interactive dashboards are dynamic visualizations that allow users to explore data interactively, filtering and drilling down to gain deeper insights.

Dashboard tools like Tableau, Power BI, or custom-built web applications are valuable for creating actionable intelligence dashboards tailored to specific needs.

Advanced visualizations, such as 3D graphs, animations, or virtual reality (VR) visualizations, offer immersive experiences that can enhance the understanding of complex data.

These advanced techniques are particularly relevant in fields like scientific research, engineering, or simulations.

Visualizing OSINT data involves selecting the most suitable visualization method based on the nature of the data and the insights you aim to extract.

It's essential to consider the target audience's familiarity with data visualization and choose methods that effectively communicate the actionable intelligence.

Moreover, combining multiple visualization techniques can provide a more comprehensive view of the data, allowing for deeper analysis and better-informed decisions.

Choosing the right visualization tools is equally crucial.

Many software applications and libraries are available for creating and customizing visualizations.

Data visualization software like Tableau, Microsoft Power BI, Google Data Studio, or open-source tools like D3.js offer a range of options for creating actionable intelligence visuals.

Geospatial visualization tools like ArcGIS or QGIS are invaluable for mapping and analyzing location-based OSINT data.

Python libraries like Matplotlib, Seaborn, Plotly, or Bokeh are widely used for creating custom data visualizations.

Machine learning and AI-driven visualization tools are emerging, leveraging algorithms to automatically select the most suitable visualization methods based on the data and goals.

Incorporating these tools into the OSINT workflow can enhance the efficiency of actionable intelligence extraction.

Collaboration and sharing of visualized data are crucial aspects of the OSINT process.

Visualizations should be accessible to all relevant stakeholders, including team members, decision-makers, and partners.

Providing clear annotations, explanations, and context within the visualizations ensures that actionable intelligence is understood and can be acted upon effectively.

Furthermore, data security and privacy considerations must be addressed when sharing visualized OSINT data.

Sensitive information should be appropriately redacted or anonymized to protect individuals' privacy and comply with legal and ethical standards.

In summary, visualizing OSINT data is a pivotal step in transforming raw information into actionable intelligence.

By employing various visualization methods and tools, analysts can simplify complex data, identify patterns, and convey insights effectively to decision-makers.

Choosing the right visualization techniques, considering the audience, and incorporating collaboration and privacy measures are essential elements of the OSINT visualization process.

Ultimately, actionable intelligence derived from well-executed visualizations can drive informed decisions, improve security measures, and contribute to the success of various endeavors in the world of open-source intelligence.

Chapter 8: Ethical Considerations and Legal Expertise

Navigating the ethical landscape in open-source intelligence (OSINT) is a complex and essential aspect of conducting responsible and lawful investigations.

Ethical considerations are at the core of OSINT operations, ensuring that information is gathered, analyzed, and used in a manner that respects privacy, legality, and the principles of responsible intelligence gathering.

Next, we will explore the multifaceted ethical challenges that OSINT practitioners encounter and the guidelines that help maintain ethical integrity in the field.

Ethical considerations in OSINT encompass a wide range of issues, including privacy, consent, legality, transparency, accuracy, and the potential consequences of information disclosure.

Balancing the need for information with ethical principles is crucial to ensuring that OSINT operations are conducted with integrity and respect for individuals' rights.

One of the fundamental ethical principles in OSINT is the respect for privacy.

Individuals have a right to privacy, and OSINT practitioners must be mindful of this right when collecting and analyzing information.

It is essential to differentiate between public information that is readily accessible and private information that requires consent or legal authorization for access.

Consent is another critical ethical aspect of OSINT.

When gathering information, particularly from online sources or social media, practitioners should respect individuals' consent preferences.

If information is intended for public consumption, such as social media posts, it may be considered consented for collection.

However, data that is not publicly accessible should not be collected without explicit consent or a legal basis.

Legal considerations are paramount in the ethical landscape of OSINT.

Practitioners must ensure that their activities comply with applicable laws and regulations, including data protection laws and regulations related to digital surveillance and online investigations.

Violating the law not only poses legal risks but also undermines the ethical foundation of OSINT.

Transparency is a guiding principle that helps maintain ethical integrity in OSINT.

Being transparent about the purpose of data collection and the sources used is essential in building trust and accountability.

Practitioners should clearly communicate their intentions when gathering information and be open about their methods.

Accuracy is a fundamental ethical principle in OSINT.

It is essential to ensure that the information collected and disseminated is accurate, reliable, and free from bias.

Errors or inaccuracies in OSINT can lead to misinformation and harm individuals' reputations or privacy.

Therefore, rigorous fact-checking and verification processes are essential to maintain ethical standards.

The principle of minimizing harm is integral to ethical OSINT practices.

Practitioners should strive to minimize any potential harm that may result from their actions, such as harm to individuals' privacy, reputation, or safety.

This principle encourages responsible decision-making in the collection and use of information.

Another ethical consideration in OSINT is the potential for unintended consequences.

Information collected and disseminated through OSINT can have far-reaching consequences, including legal, social, or personal ramifications.

Practitioners should anticipate and evaluate these potential consequences when conducting OSINT activities.

Responsible information sharing is an ethical imperative in OSINT.

Practitioners should be cautious about sharing sensitive or personal information and ensure that information is shared only with authorized individuals or organizations that have a legitimate need for it.

Unauthorized disclosure of sensitive information can have severe ethical and legal implications.

Ethical OSINT practitioners understand the importance of context in interpreting information.

Information gathered without context can lead to misinterpretation or the drawing of incorrect conclusions.

It is crucial to consider the broader context of information and avoid making unwarranted assumptions.

The ethical landscape of OSINT is dynamic, with evolving challenges and considerations in the digital age.

Practitioners must stay informed about changes in laws, regulations, and ethical guidelines relevant to OSINT.

Continuing education and professional development are essential for maintaining ethical competence.

The principle of accountability is central to ethical OSINT practices.

Practitioners should be accountable for their actions and decisions throughout the OSINT process.

This includes documenting their methods, sources, and findings, which can be valuable for transparency and auditability.

Ethical OSINT practitioners are aware of the potential for bias in information collection and analysis.

They strive to minimize bias by using diverse sources, cross-referencing information, and critically assessing their own assumptions and perspectives.

Respecting cultural and ethical norms is also crucial when conducting OSINT in different regions or among diverse populations.

Practitioners should be aware of cultural sensitivities and ethical considerations specific to the communities they are researching.

In summary, navigating the ethical landscape in OSINT is a complex and ever-evolving challenge.

Practitioners must adhere to ethical principles that prioritize privacy, consent, legality, transparency, accuracy, and minimizing harm.

Maintaining ethical integrity in OSINT is essential not only for legal compliance but also for building trust, ensuring responsible intelligence gathering, and promoting accountability.

By upholding these ethical principles, OSINT practitioners contribute to the responsible and ethical use of open-source information for legitimate purposes.

Legal compliance is a fundamental aspect of any open-source intelligence (OSINT) operation, requiring practitioners to adhere to applicable laws, regulations, and best practices.

Operating within the bounds of the law is essential to avoid legal repercussions and maintain ethical integrity in OSINT activities.

This chapter explores the legal framework surrounding OSINT, providing guidance on navigating the complex landscape of legal compliance and best practices.

OSINT practitioners must be familiar with and adhere to the legal frameworks governing their activities in their respective jurisdictions.

Laws and regulations related to OSINT can vary significantly from one country to another, and it is the responsibility of practitioners to stay informed about the relevant legal requirements.

One of the critical aspects of legal compliance in OSINT is data protection and privacy laws.

These laws dictate how personal data should be handled, processed, and protected.

Practitioners must understand and adhere to these regulations to ensure that the collection and processing of personal information are done in a lawful and ethical manner.

In many regions, the General Data Protection Regulation (GDPR) has a significant impact on OSINT operations, as it imposes strict requirements on the handling of personal data.

Under the GDPR, individuals have the right to know how their data is used, and they must provide consent for its processing.

Practitioners must respect these rights and seek explicit consent when collecting and processing personal data.

Additionally, the GDPR requires practitioners to ensure the security and confidentiality of data to prevent data breaches and unauthorized access.

Data protection impact assessments may also be necessary in certain cases to evaluate and mitigate the risks associated with data processing.

Intellectual property laws are another critical aspect of legal compliance in OSINT.

Practitioners must respect copyright and trademark laws when using information from publicly available sources.

Copying, distributing, or using copyrighted material without proper authorization can lead to legal consequences.

Fair use provisions may apply in some cases, but practitioners should exercise caution and seek legal advice if unsure about the legality of using specific content.

OSINT practitioners must also be mindful of laws related to digital surveillance and online investigations.

Many jurisdictions have specific laws that govern the use of surveillance techniques, such as web scraping, data mining, and social media monitoring.

These laws can vary greatly, and practitioners must ensure that their activities comply with local regulations.

For example, some countries have stringent rules regarding the collection and analysis of online communications data.

Failure to comply with these regulations can result in legal action and reputational damage.

It is crucial for OSINT practitioners to obtain explicit consent or use legal channels when conducting more invasive investigations.

In some cases, law enforcement or government agencies may be involved in OSINT operations, and practitioners should be aware of the legal requirements and protocols when collaborating with these entities.

Transparency and accountability are essential in maintaining legal compliance.

Practitioners should document their methods, sources, and findings in a clear and organized manner, which can be valuable for legal defense and audit purposes.

In cases where OSINT findings are used as evidence in legal proceedings, ensuring the integrity and admissibility of the evidence is critical.

Practitioners should be prepared to testify and provide evidence in court if necessary.

Adhering to best practices in OSINT is not only about legal compliance but also about maintaining ethical standards and ensuring the responsible use of open-source information.

Ethical best practices, such as respecting privacy, obtaining consent, minimizing harm, and verifying information, should be integrated into the OSINT workflow.

OSINT practitioners should also prioritize accuracy and objectivity in their investigations, avoiding bias and unsubstantiated claims.

Moreover, collaboration and information sharing within the OSINT community can help practitioners stay informed about legal developments, share best practices, and collectively address ethical and legal challenges.

In summary, legal compliance and best practices are paramount in the field of open-source intelligence.

Practitioners must be well-versed in the legal requirements and regulations governing their activities, including data protection, intellectual property, and surveillance laws.

Maintaining transparency, accountability, and ethical integrity ensures that OSINT operations are conducted responsibly and within the bounds of the law.

By adhering to legal and ethical standards, OSINT practitioners contribute to the responsible and lawful use of open-source information for legitimate purposes, while also mitigating legal risks and upholding their professional reputation.

Chapter 9: Elite Commandos in Action: Real-World OSINT Scenarios

Case studies of elite open-source intelligence (OSINT) operations provide valuable insights into the practical application of advanced OSINT techniques and methodologies.

These real-world examples illustrate the capabilities of expert OSINT practitioners and showcase the impact of OSINT in various domains and scenarios.

Next, we delve into several case studies to highlight the effectiveness and versatility of elite OSINT operations.

Case Study 1: Corporate Espionage Prevention In this case, an elite OSINT team was hired by a multinational corporation to prevent corporate espionage. The corporation had discovered leaks of sensitive internal information, including product designs and financial data. The OSINT team employed advanced monitoring and analysis techniques to identify the source of the leaks. Through deep web and dark web investigations, they traced the leaks to an insider threat within the organization. By providing actionable intelligence to the corporation, the OSINT team helped mitigate the threat and enhance their cybersecurity measures.

Case Study 2: Anti-Terrorism Intelligence An elite OSINT unit collaborated with law enforcement agencies to gather critical intelligence on potential terrorist threats. Using advanced social media analysis and linguistic profiling, the team monitored online forums and communication channels frequented by extremists. They successfully identified individuals planning a terrorist attack and provided law enforcement with timely information, leading to the apprehension of suspects and the prevention of a potential catastrophe.

Case Study 3: Political Risk Assessment A global risk management firm engaged an elite OSINT team to assess political risks in a volatile region. The team utilized a combination of geospatial analysis, sentiment analysis, and real-time monitoring of social media trends. Their findings enabled the client to make informed decisions regarding investments, operations, and security measures in the region, ultimately safeguarding their assets and personnel.

Case Study 4: Counterintelligence Operation In a high-stakes counterintelligence operation, an elite OSINT unit was tasked with identifying foreign spies operating within a government agency. The team conducted meticulous online investigations, analyzing digital footprints, and uncovering suspicious patterns of behavior. Their findings led to the identification and expulsion of several foreign agents, safeguarding national security and preventing further breaches of classified information.

Case Study 5: Cyber Threat Attribution A cybersecurity firm enlisted the expertise of elite OSINT practitioners to attribute a sophisticated cyberattack to a specific threat actor. The OSINT team analyzed malware signatures, infrastructure patterns, and online chatter in underground forums. Their comprehensive analysis allowed the cybersecurity firm to not only attribute the attack but also develop countermeasures to defend against similar threats in the future.

Case Study 6: Due Diligence for Mergers and Acquisitions During a high-profile merger negotiation, an elite OSINT team was employed to conduct due diligence on the potential partner company. The team conducted in-depth investigations into the financial health, reputation, and hidden liabilities of the target company. Their findings provided the client with critical insights, enabling them to make an informed decision and negotiate favorable terms.

Case Study 7: Human Trafficking Investigation Law enforcement agencies combating human trafficking sought the assistance of an elite OSINT unit to locate and rescue victims. The team used geolocation data, social media analysis, and advanced search techniques to track the movements of traffickers and victims. Their efforts led to the successful rescue of multiple victims and the dismantling of a human trafficking network.

Case Study 8: Competitive Intelligence In a highly competitive industry, a leading corporation engaged an elite OSINT team to gather competitive intelligence on rival companies. The team employed advanced web scraping, data analysis, and social media monitoring to track competitors' product launches, marketing strategies, and customer sentiments. The insights provided the client with a strategic advantage, allowing them to adapt and stay ahead in the market.

Case Study 9: Missing Persons Search A family desperate to locate a missing loved one turned to an elite OSINT group for help. Using publicly available information, including social media profiles, online activity, and geolocation data, the team was able to pinpoint the missing person's last known whereabouts. Their efforts led to the safe recovery of the individual and a heartfelt reunion with their family.

Case Study 10: Financial Fraud Investigation A financial institution faced a series of fraudulent transactions that threatened its stability. An elite OSINT team was tasked with identifying the culprits and their methods. By tracing cryptocurrency transactions, analyzing financial records, and monitoring online forums used by cybercriminals, the team uncovered a sophisticated fraud network. Their findings enabled the financial institution to recover stolen funds and strengthen its cybersecurity defenses.

These case studies demonstrate the diverse applications and impact of elite OSINT operations across different sectors and scenarios.

Expert OSINT practitioners leverage advanced tools, techniques, and analytical skills to address complex challenges, protect national security, enhance corporate resilience, and provide critical insights for decision-making.

Their ability to extract actionable intelligence from vast amounts of open-source data underscores the significance of OSINT in the modern information landscape.

Tackling complex open-source intelligence (OSINT) challenges requires a deep understanding of the field's nuances and the ability to adapt to evolving digital landscapes.

These challenges often involve sifting through vast amounts of publicly available data, identifying relevant information, and piecing together disparate clues to create a comprehensive intelligence picture.

Next, we explore various strategies and techniques for addressing complex OSINT challenges and offer insights into how experts navigate these intricate tasks.

One of the fundamental aspects of tackling complex OSINT challenges is having a well-defined objective.

Whether it's uncovering a cyber threat, investigating corporate fraud, or tracking individuals of interest, a clear and specific goal helps guide the entire OSINT operation.

Once the objective is established, OSINT practitioners must determine the scope of the task at hand.

Complex challenges may involve multiple layers of information, numerous data sources, and intricate patterns of behavior.

Understanding the scope allows practitioners to allocate resources effectively and plan their investigative approach.

In many cases, complex OSINT challenges require a multidisciplinary approach.

Experts with diverse skill sets, including data analysis, linguistics, cybersecurity, and digital forensics, may collaborate to tackle these challenges comprehensively.

Collaboration also extends to leveraging the capabilities of advanced OSINT tools and technologies.

While experts play a crucial role, cutting-edge software can automate data collection, streamline analysis, and identify patterns that might be missed by manual methods alone.

Advanced data analytics and machine learning algorithms can sift through enormous datasets, providing valuable insights that would be impossible to uncover manually.

However, even with the assistance of technology, OSINT practitioners must exercise critical thinking and analytical skills to interpret the results and draw meaningful conclusions.

Complex OSINT challenges often involve tracking individuals or entities with a strong online presence.

This may require monitoring social media platforms, forums, and websites where relevant information may be shared.

Practitioners must be adept at identifying online personas, recognizing patterns of behavior, and distinguishing between credible sources and disinformation.

In some cases, OSINT professionals may need to delve into the dark web, a hidden part of the internet known for its anonymity and illegal activities.

Navigating the dark web requires specialized tools and techniques, as well as a deep understanding of its dynamics and risks.

Moreover, ethical considerations are paramount when tackling complex OSINT challenges.

Practitioners must adhere to strict ethical guidelines, respecting individuals' privacy and rights while conducting investigations.

Obtaining consent, protecting sensitive data, and minimizing harm are essential principles that should guide all OSINT operations, especially in complex cases.

As the digital landscape evolves, so do the challenges faced by OSINT practitioners.

Complex challenges may involve the rapid spread of disinformation, the use of encryption to hide communication, or the manipulation of online narratives.

To address these issues, OSINT professionals must stay informed about emerging threats and adapt their techniques accordingly.

In addition to monitoring online activities, practitioners should be vigilant about safeguarding their own digital security.

Complex OSINT challenges may attract the attention of adversaries seeking to disrupt investigations or compromise the security of OSINT practitioners.

Implementing robust cybersecurity measures and practicing operational security (OPSEC) are essential for protecting sensitive information and maintaining the integrity of the operation.

Moreover, practitioners should continually update their skills and knowledge through training, workshops, and networking within the OSINT community.

Staying connected with peers and sharing insights and best practices can provide valuable support when tackling complex challenges.

In summary, tackling complex OSINT challenges requires a combination of clear objectives, multidisciplinary expertise, advanced technology, critical thinking, ethical considerations, and adaptability.

OSINT practitioners must approach these challenges with diligence, professionalism, and a commitment to upholding ethical standards.

By doing so, they can successfully navigate the intricate landscape of open-source intelligence, uncover valuable insights, and contribute to the broader goals of national security, corporate resilience, and informed decision-making.

Chapter 10: Becoming an Elite OSINT Commando: Challenges and Achievements

The journey to becoming an elite open-source intelligence (OSINT) practitioner is marked by numerous challenges and obstacles that require determination, resilience, and continuous learning.

As you progress along this path, you will encounter challenges that test your skills, knowledge, and ethical principles.

One of the initial hurdles you may face is information overload.

The vastness of the internet and the sheer volume of publicly available data can be overwhelming, making it difficult to discern what is relevant and valuable for your OSINT objectives.

To overcome this challenge, you must develop effective filtering and prioritization techniques to focus your efforts on the most pertinent information.

Another common challenge is maintaining anonymity and operational security (OPSEC) while conducting OSINT investigations.

As you delve deeper into online communities and forums, you may attract attention from adversaries who seek to uncover your identity or disrupt your activities.

Implementing robust OPSEC measures, such as using virtual private networks (VPNs), secure communication channels, and anonymous online personas, is essential to protect your identity and maintain the integrity of your investigations.

Ethical considerations are a critical aspect of OSINT work, and navigating the ethical landscape can be challenging.

You may encounter situations where the lines between ethical and unethical behavior are blurred.

Balancing the need for information with respect for privacy and legality is a constant challenge for OSINT practitioners.

To overcome this challenge, it is essential to adhere to a strict code of ethics, seek legal guidance when necessary, and always prioritize the protection of individuals' rights and privacy.

In the pursuit of elite status in OSINT, continuous learning and skill development are paramount.

Technology evolves rapidly, and new tools, techniques, and platforms emerge regularly.

Staying up-to-date with the latest developments in the field and expanding your skill set through training and certifications is essential to maintain your competitive edge.

Collaboration can be both a challenge and an opportunity on the path to elite status.

While working with other OSINT practitioners can enhance your capabilities, it can also be challenging to find trusted partners and build effective collaborative relationships.

Overcoming this challenge requires networking within the OSINT community, building trust, and fostering productive partnerships based on shared goals and values.

Resource limitations, such as access to premium OSINT tools and data sources, can hinder your progress toward elite status.

These resources often come at a cost, and not all practitioners have the financial means to invest in them.

To address this challenge, consider exploring open-source alternatives, participating in OSINT communities that share resources, and leveraging free or trial versions of premium tools whenever possible.

Complex and evolving threats in the digital landscape pose significant challenges for OSINT practitioners.

Adversaries continually adapt their tactics, techniques, and procedures (TTPs) to evade detection and maintain anonymity.

Staying one step ahead of these threats requires a deep understanding of cybersecurity, threat intelligence, and advanced OSINT techniques.

Intricate investigations involving the analysis of encrypted communications, hidden services on the dark web, or complex financial transactions can be particularly challenging for OSINT practitioners.

These cases demand advanced technical skills, specialized tools, and a high level of expertise to unravel the complexities and provide meaningful insights.

Maintaining a high level of professionalism and commitment to ethical principles is essential when overcoming challenges on the path to elite status.

The actions and decisions of OSINT practitioners have real-world consequences, and upholding ethical standards is non-negotiable.

Acting with integrity, respecting privacy, and adhering to legal and ethical guidelines should be at the forefront of your practice.

The path to elite status in OSINT is not without its setbacks and failures.

You may encounter investigations that do not yield the desired results, encounter resistance from adversaries, or face legal and ethical dilemmas.

However, it is essential to view these challenges as opportunities for growth and learning.

Each setback can provide valuable lessons and insights that contribute to your development as an elite OSINT practitioner.

To overcome these challenges, it is crucial to cultivate a growth mindset, embrace a commitment to continuous improvement, and learn from both your successes and failures.

In summary, the path to elite status in open-source intelligence is fraught with challenges that demand a combination of technical expertise, ethical integrity, continuous learning, and a resilient mindset.

Navigating the complexities of the digital landscape while upholding ethical standards requires dedication and perseverance.

By embracing these challenges as opportunities for growth and development, you can progress toward elite status and make a meaningful impact in the field of OSINT.

The world of elite open-source intelligence (OSINT) commandos is one of continuous learning and dedication, where practitioners are committed to mastering the art of information gathering and analysis.

As you journey through the realm of OSINT, you'll inevitably encounter numerous milestones and achievements that mark your progress.

These achievements reflect your growth as an OSINT professional and serve as a testament to your dedication and expertise.

One of the earliest achievements in your OSINT journey is gaining proficiency in essential OSINT tools and techniques.

This milestone signifies your ability to navigate the digital landscape, extract valuable information, and apply basic analysis skills to make sense of the data you collect.

It's a foundational step toward becoming an effective OSINT practitioner.

As you continue to develop your skills, you'll reach the point where you can confidently perform complex OSINT investigations.

These investigations may involve tracking individuals or entities across various online platforms, analyzing their digital footprint, and uncovering hidden insights.

Achieving success in these investigations is a significant milestone on your path to elite status.

Another crucial achievement is mastering the use of advanced OSINT tools and technologies.

These tools can streamline your workflow, automate data collection, and provide advanced analytics capabilities.

Becoming proficient in these tools enhances your efficiency and effectiveness as an OSINT commando.

Collaboration is a fundamental aspect of OSINT, and building strong partnerships with trusted colleagues and organizations is a noteworthy achievement.

Working together with like-minded professionals allows you to leverage collective expertise and resources, expanding your capabilities beyond what you can achieve alone.

Becoming a respected and trusted member of the OSINT community is an achievement that signifies your commitment to ethical conduct and professionalism.

Your reputation as an OSINT practitioner who upholds high ethical standards and respects privacy is invaluable in the field.

Delving into complex investigations, such as cyber threat intelligence or financial analysis, represents another significant milestone in your OSINT journey.

These investigations require advanced technical skills, critical thinking, and expertise in specialized areas, showcasing your versatility as an OSINT commando.

Contributing to real-world outcomes and making a tangible impact with your OSINT skills is a gratifying achievement.

Whether it's assisting law enforcement in solving a cybercrime or providing actionable intelligence to a corporate client, your ability to effect change through OSINT is a testament to your expertise.

Earning recognition from peers and organizations in the OSINT community is a noteworthy achievement.

Awards, certifications, and invitations to speak at conferences or join advisory boards validate your expertise and contributions to the field.

Becoming a mentor to aspiring OSINT practitioners and sharing your knowledge with the next generation is a rewarding achievement.

It allows you to give back to the community, nurture new talent, and contribute to the ongoing growth of the OSINT field.

Receiving accolades and acknowledgments from clients, employers, or agencies for your OSINT contributions is a gratifying milestone.

It demonstrates the practical value of your skills and reaffirms your importance in the world of information gathering and analysis.

In summary, the world of elite OSINT commandos is a dynamic and ever-evolving realm where achievements mark your progress and contributions.

From mastering essential skills to becoming a respected member of the OSINT community and making a tangible impact on investigations and organizations, each achievement is a testament to your dedication and expertise.

Embracing these milestones with humility and a commitment to continuous growth allows you to thrive in the world of elite OSINT practitioners.

BOOK 4
EXPERT STRATEGIES IN OSINT COMMANDO UNLOCKING SECRETS AT EVERY SKILL LEVEL

ROB BOTWRIGHT

Chapter 1: The OSINT Commando Spectrum

In the world of open-source intelligence (OSINT), expertise is not a one-size-fits-all concept; rather, it encompasses a range of levels, each requiring a unique set of skills and knowledge.

These levels of expertise are akin to stepping stones, with each one building upon the foundation of the previous.

At the entry level, individuals are just beginning their OSINT journey, often guided by curiosity and a desire to learn.

They are eager to explore the vast landscape of publicly available information and understand its potential applications.

At this stage, beginners focus on mastering the basics, such as effective search engine queries and simple data collection techniques.

They may not yet have a clear specialization and are in the process of discovering their specific interests within the OSINT field.

As beginners gain experience and confidence, they progress to the intermediate level of OSINT expertise.

At this stage, practitioners start to refine their skills and deepen their understanding of OSINT tools and methodologies.

They become proficient in using a variety of online resources, such as social media platforms, public records databases, and specialized search engines.

Intermediate OSINT practitioners are capable of conducting more in-depth investigations and uncovering valuable insights from the information they gather.

They also begin to develop a focus or specialization within the field, whether it be in cyber threat intelligence, digital forensics, or online reputation management.

The advanced level of OSINT expertise represents a significant leap in skill and knowledge.

Practitioners at this stage have honed their abilities to a high degree of proficiency.

They possess a deep understanding of complex OSINT tools and techniques, allowing them to tackle intricate investigations with ease.

Advanced OSINT experts are often sought after for their specialized knowledge in areas such as dark web research, cryptocurrency analysis, or geospatial intelligence.

They are also adept at data analysis, visualization, and interpretation, enabling them to provide actionable intelligence to clients and organizations.

Beyond advanced expertise lies the realm of elite OSINT practitioners.

These individuals have achieved the highest level of mastery in the field, demonstrating unparalleled skill and knowledge.

They are the trailblazers and innovators, pushing the boundaries of what is possible in the world of OSINT.

Elite OSINT practitioners often contribute to the development of new tools and methodologies, shaping the future of the field.

They are sought after by government agencies, law enforcement, private corporations, and other organizations for their ability to provide critical intelligence and solve complex problems.

Becoming an elite OSINT practitioner is not only a matter of technical proficiency but also a commitment to ethical conduct and a deep respect for privacy and legality.

These experts are acutely aware of the ethical dilemmas that can arise in OSINT work and navigate them with integrity.

They prioritize the protection of individuals' rights and privacy while delivering accurate and actionable intelligence. The path to elite OSINT expertise is marked by continuous learning and growth.

Practitioners at all levels of expertise must stay up-to-date with the latest developments in technology, cybersecurity, and online platforms.

They must also cultivate a growth mindset, embracing challenges as opportunities for improvement.

Mentorship and collaboration play a vital role in advancing through the levels of OSINT expertise.

Established experts often guide and mentor those at lower levels, sharing their knowledge and experience.

Collaborating with peers in the OSINT community allows practitioners to pool resources, tackle complex investigations, and gain new perspectives.

In summary, the journey through the levels of OSINT expertise is a dynamic and rewarding process.

From beginners exploring the possibilities of OSINT to elite practitioners shaping the future of the field, each level represents a unique stage of growth and development.

Regardless of their current level, OSINT practitioners share a common passion for uncovering hidden information and providing valuable insights to support decision-making and investigations.

In the ever-evolving landscape of intelligence and security, the role of open-source intelligence (OSINT) commandos has gained prominence and significance.

These highly skilled professionals play a vital role in gathering, analyzing, and disseminating information from publicly available sources to support various intelligence and security efforts.

The modern world is characterized by an abundance of digital data, much of which is accessible to anyone with an internet connection.

This data encompasses a wide range of sources, including social media platforms, news articles, online forums, public records, and more.

OSINT commandos are individuals who harness the power of this publicly available information to provide valuable insights to their organizations or clients.

Their role is multifaceted and essential in today's information-driven society.

One of the primary responsibilities of OSINT commandos is to monitor and analyze online conversations and activities.

They keep a watchful eye on social media platforms, forums, and chat rooms to identify emerging trends, threats, or opportunities.

This real-time monitoring allows organizations to stay ahead of potential crises, adapt to changing circumstances, and make informed decisions.

OSINT commandos are also tasked with conducting investigations and research on individuals, organizations, or entities of interest.

They use a variety of tools and techniques to collect information about these subjects, helping their organizations assess risks, make strategic decisions, or support law enforcement efforts.

The intelligence gathered by OSINT professionals often complements classified information obtained through traditional intelligence channels.

One of the defining features of OSINT is its open and transparent nature.

OSINT commandos rely on publicly available sources and adhere to ethical guidelines to ensure that their activities respect privacy and legal boundaries.

Their work is characterized by transparency, and they do not engage in hacking, illegal data access, or any activities that infringe upon individuals' rights or violate laws.

In the realm of cybersecurity, OSINT commandos play a crucial role in threat intelligence.

They monitor online forums and communities where cybercriminals exchange information, vulnerabilities, and malware.

By staying informed about potential threats, they help organizations fortify their defenses and respond proactively to cyberattacks.

Another vital aspect of the OSINT commando's role is information verification and validation.

In an era of misinformation and fake news, OSINT professionals are trained to assess the credibility and authenticity of information they encounter.

Their ability to distinguish between accurate and false information is essential in preventing the spread of misinformation and ensuring that decision-makers rely on reliable data.

OSINT commandos often work in diverse settings, including government agencies, law enforcement, corporate security, and private intelligence firms.

Their skills and expertise are in high demand across various sectors, as organizations recognize the value of OSINT in gaining a competitive edge, mitigating risks, and safeguarding their interests.

The role of OSINT commandos is not limited to reactive measures; they also contribute to proactive intelligence strategies.

By monitoring online discussions and trends, they can identify potential threats or opportunities before they fully materialize.

This proactive approach enables organizations to take preemptive actions to mitigate risks or seize advantageous positions.

Furthermore, OSINT commandos are crucial in conducting due diligence and background checks.

Whether it's vetting potential business partners, employees, or investment opportunities, their investigative skills help organizations make informed choices and avoid potential pitfalls.

In recent years, OSINT has gained recognition as an invaluable tool in the field of competitive intelligence.

Companies use OSINT to gain insights into their competitors' strategies, market positioning, and customer sentiment.

This information allows them to fine-tune their own strategies, respond to market changes, and maintain a competitive edge.

As the digital landscape continues to evolve, the role of OSINT commandos is expected to expand and adapt.

The integration of advanced technologies, such as artificial intelligence and machine learning, into OSINT tools will further enhance their capabilities.

Moreover, the increasing interconnectedness of the online world means that OSINT professionals must be vigilant and adaptable in identifying emerging threats and opportunities.

In summary, OSINT commandos are indispensable assets in the modern intelligence and security ecosystem.

Their ability to harness publicly available information, adhere to ethical guidelines, and provide timely and accurate intelligence is essential in safeguarding organizations' interests and responding to the challenges of the digital age.

Chapter 2: Mastering the Fundamentals: A Deep Dive

To become proficient in open-source intelligence (OSINT), it's essential to deepen your understanding of its fundamentals.

OSINT is a multifaceted discipline that relies on the collection, analysis, and interpretation of publicly available information.

At its core, OSINT seeks to transform raw data into actionable intelligence that can inform decision-making and investigations.

One fundamental aspect of OSINT is the concept of open sources.

These sources encompass a wide range of publicly available information, including data from the internet, print media, public records, and more.

Open sources are distinct from classified or restricted information and are accessible to anyone who knows where to look.

Understanding the nature of open sources is crucial because it defines the scope of OSINT and the types of data that OSINT practitioners work with.

Another key element of OSINT is the principle of transparency.

OSINT is conducted in an open and transparent manner, adhering to ethical guidelines and legal boundaries.

Practitioners must ensure that their activities respect privacy, legality, and individual rights.

Ethical considerations are paramount in OSINT, and professionals must navigate potential ethical dilemmas with integrity and responsibility.

Furthermore, OSINT relies on a diverse set of tools and techniques to gather and analyze information.

These tools can range from basic search engines and web scraping scripts to specialized OSINT software and data analysis platforms.

Proficiency in using these tools is essential for effective OSINT work, and practitioners often develop their expertise through continuous learning and hands-on experience.

The process of OSINT typically begins with the identification of information needs and objectives.

What specific information does an organization or investigator require, and what are the goals of the OSINT operation?

Clarity in defining these objectives is essential, as it guides the entire OSINT process.

Once objectives are established, OSINT professionals embark on the collection phase.

This phase involves accessing and retrieving relevant information from open sources.

Practitioners may use various search techniques, such as keyword searches, data mining, and social media monitoring, to gather data.

During the collection phase, it's crucial to verify the credibility and authenticity of the information obtained.

Misinformation and false data can easily spread in the digital age, so OSINT professionals must exercise caution and critical thinking.

Once collected, the data is subjected to analysis and evaluation.

This phase involves examining the information in-depth, identifying patterns, relationships, and anomalies, and assessing its significance.

Effective data analysis is a cornerstone of OSINT, as it transforms raw data into actionable intelligence.

Visualizing the results of data analysis is another vital aspect of OSINT.

Visualization tools and techniques help convey complex information in a clear and understandable manner.

Charts, graphs, maps, and timelines can all be used to present OSINT findings to decision-makers or stakeholders.

Throughout the entire OSINT process, practitioners must maintain meticulous records and documentation.

This not only ensures transparency and accountability but also aids in the replication of findings and the auditing of the OSINT operation.

The dissemination of OSINT intelligence is the final step in the process.

The information and insights derived from OSINT must be conveyed to the relevant parties in a timely and effective manner.

This often involves preparing reports, briefings, or presentations that convey the key findings and recommendations.

In addition to the technical aspects of OSINT, understanding the human element is crucial.

OSINT professionals must possess strong critical thinking skills, adaptability, and a keen understanding of human behavior and psychology.

This is especially relevant when analyzing social media data or online communities, where human interactions and motivations play a significant role.

Moreover, OSINT practitioners must stay up-to-date with the evolving digital landscape.

New online platforms, technologies, and communication methods continually emerge, and OSINT professionals must adapt to these changes to remain effective.

Furthermore, legal and ethical considerations in OSINT are paramount.

Professionals must be well-versed in the laws and regulations governing the collection and use of open-source information.

Respecting privacy, adhering to copyright laws, and avoiding illegal or unethical activities are fundamental principles of OSINT.

In summary, deepening your understanding of OSINT fundamentals is a continuous journey that combines technical skills, ethical awareness, and a holistic view of the intelligence process.

OSINT is a dynamic field that plays a vital role in various domains, from cybersecurity and law enforcement to business intelligence and national security.

By mastering its fundamentals, practitioners can harness the power of open sources to gather intelligence, make informed decisions, and contribute to the safety and security of individuals and organizations in the digital age.

In the realm of open-source intelligence (OSINT), developing a strong foundation is the first step toward expertise.

A solid foundation serves as the bedrock upon which you can build your skills and capabilities in this dynamic field.

Whether you are a novice just starting your journey or an experienced practitioner looking to refine your abilities, the importance of a strong foundation cannot be overstated.

At its core, a strong foundation in OSINT begins with a comprehensive understanding of its principles and methodologies.

This understanding includes recognizing the sources of open-source information, the legal and ethical considerations, and the various techniques used to collect and analyze data.

With this knowledge in hand, you can navigate the complexities of OSINT effectively and responsibly.A key aspect of developing a strong foundation in OSINT is familiarizing yourself with the vast landscape of open sources. These sources encompass a wide range of publicly available information, such as websites, social media platforms, news articles, public records, and more. Becoming adept at identifying and accessing these sources is fundamental to OSINT work. Additionally, understanding the limitations and biases inherent in open sources is crucial. Not all information available in the public domain is accurate, reliable, or unbiased, and recognizing these limitations is essential for discerning truth from misinformation.

A strong foundation in OSINT also involves cultivating critical thinking skills.

OSINT practitioners must approach data with a critical mindset, questioning the veracity of information and considering potential biases or motives behind its dissemination.

Critical thinking enables you to assess the credibility of sources, spot inconsistencies, and draw meaningful conclusions from the data you encounter.

Furthermore, OSINT is not a one-size-fits-all discipline, and a strong foundation involves tailoring your skills to your specific objectives.

Whether your goal is to conduct investigations, support cybersecurity efforts, or inform strategic decision-making, understanding how to adapt your OSINT techniques to your mission is essential.

The development of technical skills is another pivotal component of building a strong foundation in OSINT.

This includes proficiency in using OSINT tools, software, and platforms that facilitate data collection and analysis.

Command of these tools allows you to work efficiently and extract meaningful insights from the vast sea of open-source information.

As you develop your technical skills, it's essential to stay current with the evolving landscape of OSINT tools and technologies.

The field is dynamic, with new tools and techniques emerging regularly, and keeping up-to-date ensures that your skill set remains relevant and effective.

In addition to technical skills, effective communication is a fundamental element of OSINT expertise.

The ability to convey your findings and insights to others, whether through written reports, oral presentations, or visualizations, is essential.

Clear and concise communication ensures that the intelligence you gather is understood and actionable by decision-makers or stakeholders.

Furthermore, developing a strong foundation involves a commitment to ongoing learning and professional growth.

OSINT is a field that continually evolves, and maintaining expertise requires staying informed about emerging trends, threats, and opportunities.

This may involve attending training, participating in OSINT communities, or pursuing certifications relevant to your specialization.

Ethical considerations are a critical aspect of building a strong foundation in OSINT.

Practitioners must operate within ethical boundaries, respecting individual privacy and legal regulations.

Understanding the ethical guidelines and principles that govern OSINT ensures that your work is conducted responsibly and ethically.

Building a strong foundation in OSINT also entails honing your investigative skills.

Whether you are conducting background checks, analyzing social media data, or tracking online communities, investigative techniques are central to OSINT work.

These skills enable you to uncover hidden insights, connect dots, and draw meaningful conclusions from disparate pieces of information.

Moreover, a strong foundation in OSINT includes an appreciation for the multidisciplinary nature of the field.

OSINT draws from various disciplines, including information technology, psychology, sociology, and more.

Recognizing the interconnectedness of these disciplines allows you to approach OSINT with a holistic perspective and address complex challenges effectively.

In summary, developing a strong foundation in open-source intelligence is a multifaceted endeavor that encompasses knowledge, skills, ethics, and adaptability.

It is the cornerstone upon which expertise is built, enabling practitioners to navigate the complexities of the field and provide valuable insights to support various missions and objectives.

Whether you are just beginning your journey in OSINT or seeking to enhance your existing skills, a strong foundation serves as the springboard for success in this dynamic and vital discipline.

Chapter 3: Advanced Spokeo Techniques for Experts

In the realm of open-source intelligence (OSINT), Spokeo stands out as a versatile and powerful tool for advanced search and analysis.

As you delve deeper into the world of OSINT, understanding how to harness Spokeo's advanced capabilities becomes essential.

Spokeo's interface may seem deceptively simple at first glance, but beneath its user-friendly exterior lies a treasure trove of tools and features for OSINT professionals.

One of the key strengths of Spokeo is its ability to aggregate data from various sources, providing a comprehensive view of an individual or entity.

By entering a name, phone number, email address, or physical address, Spokeo scours the internet for relevant information, including social media profiles, public records, and online mentions.

The wealth of data retrieved by Spokeo can be invaluable for OSINT investigations, background checks, and due diligence.

To unlock Spokeo's advanced search and analysis tools, users must familiarize themselves with its search operators and filters.

These operators allow for precise and targeted searches, enabling users to narrow down results and focus on specific aspects of an individual's digital footprint.

For example, Spokeo supports operators like AND, OR, NOT, and parentheses to create complex search queries.

By combining these operators with filters such as location, age, or social media platforms, OSINT professionals can fine-tune their searches to extract the most relevant information.

Spokeo's advanced search capabilities also extend to reverse phone lookup and email search.

These features enable users to identify the owner of a phone number or an email address, potentially uncovering hidden connections or aliases.

Additionally, Spokeo provides a reverse address lookup tool, allowing users to discover information about a specific physical location, such as property details and nearby residents.

Another valuable asset in Spokeo's arsenal is its social media search functionality.

With the prevalence of social media platforms in today's digital landscape, social media searches are a vital component of OSINT investigations.

Spokeo enables users to enter a username or profile URL to retrieve information from various social media networks.

This feature can help OSINT professionals track online personas, monitor online activities, and gather valuable intelligence.

Furthermore, Spokeo offers an email lookup tool that can reveal associated social media profiles, providing a more comprehensive view of an individual's online presence.

Spokeo's versatility extends beyond individual searches; it also supports domain searches.

By entering a domain name, users can uncover information about a website, including its owner, hosting provider, and registration details.

This capability is valuable for OSINT investigations into websites, domains, or online entities.

Spokeo's analysis tools go beyond data collection; they also assist in data interpretation.

For example, Spokeo's data visualization features enable users to create charts, graphs, and maps based on the retrieved information.

These visualizations can help OSINT professionals identify trends, relationships, or geographic patterns within the data.

Additionally, Spokeo's data export options allow users to download the collected information in various formats for further analysis or reporting.

Spokeo's advanced features also extend to its notification system.

Users can set up alerts to receive real-time updates when new information related to their searches becomes available.

This proactive approach ensures that OSINT professionals stay informed about relevant developments and changes.

When using Spokeo for OSINT, it's crucial to keep ethical considerations in mind.

Respecting privacy and legal regulations is paramount, and practitioners should use the tool responsibly and within the bounds of the law.

Furthermore, OSINT professionals should verify the accuracy and authenticity of the information retrieved from Spokeo and cross-reference it with other sources when necessary.

In summary, Spokeo's advanced search and analysis tools make it a valuable asset for OSINT professionals seeking to uncover hidden insights and gather intelligence from open sources.

By mastering Spokeo's operators, filters, and features, practitioners can conduct precise and effective OSINT investigations, monitor online activities, and make informed decisions based on the data they retrieve.

However, ethical considerations and responsible use of the tool remain essential aspects of conducting OSINT with Spokeo to ensure the integrity of the information and respect for individual privacy.

As an experienced open-source intelligence (OSINT) practitioner, you recognize the importance of harnessing advanced tools like Spokeo to their fullest potential.

Leveraging Spokeo's capabilities can significantly enhance the depth and effectiveness of your OSINT investigations.

While Spokeo's basic functions are accessible to beginners, delving into its advanced features requires a deeper understanding and mastery of the tool.

One of the key advantages of Spokeo is its ability to aggregate data from an extensive range of sources.

To fully leverage this capability, you should start by conducting more sophisticated searches, utilizing various search operators and filters available within the platform.

By doing so, you can narrow down results, eliminate noise, and pinpoint the information that is most relevant to your investigation.

Spokeo's advanced search operators, including AND, OR, NOT, and parentheses, enable you to craft intricate search queries that yield precise results.

These operators can be combined with filters such as location, age, or social media platforms to focus your investigation with laser-like accuracy.

Reverse phone lookup and email search are two advanced features of Spokeo that can be invaluable in your investigations.

These tools allow you to identify the owners of phone numbers or email addresses, shedding light on hidden connections and potentially revealing aliases used by your subjects of interest.

Reverse address lookup is another advanced capability within Spokeo that you can leverage to extract detailed information about specific physical locations.

This can be particularly useful when investigating properties or individuals associated with particular addresses.

Spokeo's social media search functionality is a crucial asset for OSINT practitioners, as it allows you to track and monitor online personas and activities.

By entering a username or profile URL, you can retrieve information from a variety of social media networks, helping you build a more comprehensive profile of your subjects.

Spokeo's email lookup tool is another advanced feature that can enhance your investigations.

It not only provides information related to email addresses but also identifies associated social media profiles, offering a deeper insight into an individual's online presence.

To fully leverage Spokeo's advanced search and analysis tools, it's essential to understand the broader context of your investigation.

Consider the objectives of your inquiry and the specific information you are seeking, and then tailor your searches and queries accordingly.

Spokeo's domain search functionality is yet another advanced tool that can be beneficial when investigating websites or online entities.

By entering a domain name, you can retrieve information about the website's ownership, hosting provider, and registration details, which can be valuable in OSINT investigations.

Data visualization is a powerful feature offered by Spokeo's advanced tools.

You can create charts, graphs, and maps based on the collected information to identify trends, relationships, and geographic patterns within your data.

These visualizations provide a clearer understanding of the data and can aid in making informed decisions.

When leveraging Spokeo's advanced capabilities, it's crucial to maintain ethical standards and adhere to legal regulations.

Respect for individual privacy and responsible use of the tool should always guide your actions.

Additionally, verifying the accuracy and authenticity of the information you obtain through Spokeo is essential to ensure the integrity of your investigations.

Spokeo's data export options enable you to download collected information in various formats for further analysis or reporting.

This feature allows you to integrate the data seamlessly into your investigative processes.

Spokeo's notification system is a proactive tool that can keep you informed about relevant developments in your investigations.

Setting up alerts ensures that you stay up-to-date with any changes related to your search queries, providing a valuable advantage in dynamic OSINT operations.

In summary, leveraging Spokeo's full potential for expert investigations requires a deep understanding of its advanced features and capabilities.

By mastering search operators, filters, and analysis tools, you can conduct precise and effective OSINT investigations, monitor online activities, and make informed decisions based on the data you retrieve.

Ethical considerations and responsible use of the tool are paramount to ensure that your investigations are conducted with integrity and respect for privacy.

Ultimately, Spokeo's advanced features can empower you to uncover hidden insights, build comprehensive profiles, and extract actionable intelligence from open sources, making it an indispensable tool in the toolkit of an experienced OSINT practitioner.

Chapter 4: Spiderfoot Mastery: Expert-Level Reconnaissance

In the realm of open-source intelligence (OSINT), advanced reconnaissance is a vital component of gathering valuable information.

As you progress in your OSINT journey, mastering advanced reconnaissance strategies with tools like Spiderfoot becomes essential.

Spiderfoot's capabilities extend far beyond basic reconnaissance, and understanding how to leverage its advanced features can significantly enhance the depth and effectiveness of your investigations.

One of the strengths of Spiderfoot lies in its ability to conduct automated scans of a wide range of data sources.

To harness this power effectively, you need to develop advanced strategies for configuring and customizing your scans.

Spiderfoot allows you to tailor your scans by specifying the modules you want to use, setting scan depths, and defining scan targets.

By customizing your scans, you can focus on specific areas of interest and collect more relevant information.

Furthermore, Spiderfoot supports the use of transforms, which are custom data enrichment plugins.

These transforms can be employed to extract additional data from the information Spiderfoot retrieves, expanding your pool of intelligence.

To leverage Spiderfoot's advanced reconnaissance capabilities, you should consider the depth and breadth of your investigations.

Think about the objectives of your inquiry and the specific information you seek to uncover.

With this in mind, you can configure Spiderfoot scans to target particular aspects of your subjects of interest.

Spiderfoot's reconnaissance goes beyond the surface web; it can delve into the deep and dark web, where valuable but hidden information often resides.

By configuring Spiderfoot to include deep and dark web sources in your scans, you can uncover insights that may not be accessible through traditional search methods.

Another advanced aspect of Spiderfoot is its ability to conduct passive DNS analysis.

This technique involves analyzing historical DNS data to reveal associations, connections, and changes related to domains and IP addresses.

By incorporating passive DNS analysis into your reconnaissance strategies, you can gain a better understanding of the online infrastructure and activities of your subjects.

Furthermore, Spiderfoot supports the integration of external tools and services, enabling you to enhance your investigations even further.

By connecting Spiderfoot with additional data sources or analysis tools, you can access a broader range of information and conduct more comprehensive reconnaissance.

The power of Spiderfoot's reconnaissance lies in its ability to automate and streamline data collection.

However, it's crucial to maintain ethical standards and respect legal regulations when conducting OSINT investigations.

Ensure that your reconnaissance activities are conducted responsibly and within the bounds of the law.

Additionally, verify the accuracy and authenticity of the information you obtain through Spiderfoot by cross-referencing it with other sources when necessary.

When configuring Spiderfoot scans for advanced reconnaissance, consider the potential risks associated with your investigations.

Exercise caution when targeting sensitive or high-profile subjects, and be prepared to adapt your strategies to address unexpected challenges.

In summary, advanced reconnaissance strategies with Spiderfoot are a crucial component of OSINT investigations.

By customizing scans, utilizing transforms, and targeting specific areas of interest, you can uncover valuable insights and intelligence.

Spiderfoot's ability to access deep and dark web sources, conduct passive DNS analysis, and integrate with external tools expands your capabilities as an OSINT practitioner.

However, ethical considerations and responsible use of the tool should always guide your actions.

Maintaining respect for privacy and legal compliance is paramount to conducting reconnaissance with integrity.

With a deep understanding of Spiderfoot's advanced features and a strategic approach to your investigations, you can gather actionable intelligence and make informed decisions based on the data you retrieve, ultimately becoming a more proficient OSINT practitioner.

In the world of open-source intelligence (OSINT), expertise is measured by the depth and precision of intelligence gathering, and Spiderfoot stands as a powerful tool for those seeking to ascend to expert-level OSINT capabilities.

As you progress on your OSINT journey, it becomes increasingly important to master the intricacies of Spiderfoot's advanced features to conduct intelligence gathering at an expert level.

While Spiderfoot is accessible to beginners, its true potential shines when it is wielded by those who understand how to harness its advanced capabilities.

One of Spiderfoot's advanced features is its flexibility in configuring scans.

For expert-level intelligence gathering, it's imperative to craft highly customized scans tailored to your specific investigative objectives.

This involves selecting the most relevant modules, setting the scan depth, and defining precise scan targets that align with the scope of your inquiry.

By doing so, you can extract valuable intelligence efficiently and effectively.

Spiderfoot's ability to utilize transforms, which are custom data enrichment plugins, is another advanced facet that can elevate your intelligence gathering endeavors.

Transforms allow you to extract additional data from the information Spiderfoot retrieves, expanding your pool of insights and enhancing your analytical capabilities.

As an expert OSINT practitioner, you should utilize transforms strategically to extract hidden information and establish a comprehensive understanding of your subjects. Understanding the nuances of Spiderfoot's advanced reconnaissance capabilities is pivotal.

It enables you to access information beyond the surface web, delving into the depths of the deep and dark web where critical intelligence often resides.

Incorporating these advanced features into your intelligence gathering strategies will yield a broader and deeper spectrum of information.

Spiderfoot also offers passive DNS analysis, a feature that expert-level OSINT practitioners find invaluable.

This analysis involves dissecting historical DNS data to uncover associations, connections, and changes related to domains and IP addresses.

By incorporating passive DNS analysis into your intelligence gathering, you can uncover deeper insights into the online infrastructure and activities of your subjects.

Furthermore, Spiderfoot's integration capabilities allow you to connect it with external tools and services.

This versatility empowers you to augment your intelligence gathering efforts by accessing a wider array of data sources and analytical resources.

The synergy between Spiderfoot and external tools enhances your capacity to extract actionable intelligence and make informed decisions based on the data you gather.

While Spiderfoot's advanced features enable expert-level intelligence gathering, it is crucial to operate within ethical and legal boundaries.

Conduct your OSINT investigations responsibly and ethically, respecting individual privacy and adhering to legal regulations.

Verification of the accuracy and authenticity of the information you obtain through Spiderfoot should be a standard practice.

Cross-referencing and corroborating data from multiple sources are essential steps to ensure the reliability of your intelligence.

As you ascend to expert-level intelligence gathering with Spiderfoot, consider the potential risks associated with your investigations.

Exercise caution, particularly when dealing with sensitive subjects, and be prepared to adapt your strategies to address unexpected challenges.

In summary, expert-level intelligence gathering with Spiderfoot requires a deep understanding of its advanced features and a strategic approach to OSINT investigations.

Customizing scans, employing transforms, accessing deep and dark web sources, utilizing passive DNS analysis, and integrating external tools are essential components of an expert's toolkit.

However, ethical considerations and responsible use of the tool should always guide your actions.

Maintaining respect for privacy, legal compliance, and data verification are non-negotiable aspects of conducting expert-level intelligence gathering.

With the mastery of Spiderfoot's advanced capabilities and a commitment to ethical conduct, you can elevate your OSINT practice to expert status, extracting actionable intelligence and contributing meaningfully to your investigative objectives.

Chapter 5: SEON: Advanced Strategies for the Informed Expert

In the realm of open-source intelligence (OSINT), SEON stands as a formidable tool known for its advanced features and capabilities, making it an essential asset for those seeking to elevate their OSINT expertise.

As you progress on your OSINT journey, understanding and harnessing SEON's advanced features becomes critical to conducting in-depth investigations and extracting valuable insights.

SEON offers a range of advanced features that empower OSINT practitioners to gather intelligence with precision and efficiency.

One of SEON's standout capabilities is its ability to conduct sophisticated searches across a wide array of data sources.

For those aiming to achieve expert-level OSINT proficiency, mastering the art of crafting precise search queries within SEON is essential.

This involves utilizing advanced search operators and filters to narrow down results and target specific information relevant to your investigative objectives.

By fine-tuning your search queries, you can extract valuable intelligence more effectively.

SEON also provides the option to set up custom alerts, which is a feature cherished by advanced OSINT practitioners.

These alerts enable you to receive real-time notifications when new information matching your criteria surfaces online.

For expert-level OSINT investigations, setting up and managing custom alerts can be a game-changer, ensuring you stay up-to-date with the latest developments related to your subjects.

Another advanced aspect of SEON is its data enrichment capabilities.

SEON can automatically enrich data by pulling in additional information from various sources, thereby providing a more comprehensive view of your subjects.

As an advanced OSINT practitioner, you should explore and leverage SEON's data enrichment features to enhance your analytical capabilities and extract deeper insights.

Moreover, SEON supports the integration of external tools and services, expanding its capabilities even further.

By connecting SEON with complementary OSINT tools or data analysis platforms, you can access a broader range of data sources and analytical resources, thus elevating the depth and breadth of your investigations.

While SEON empowers OSINT practitioners to conduct advanced investigations, it is essential to operate within ethical and legal boundaries.

Responsible and ethical conduct should guide your actions throughout the investigative process.

Always respect individual privacy and adhere to legal regulations when collecting and analyzing information using SEON.

Additionally, thorough verification of the accuracy and authenticity of the data obtained through SEON is crucial.

Cross-referencing and validating information from multiple sources should be standard practice to ensure the reliability of your intelligence.

As you advance in your OSINT journey with SEON, consider the potential risks and challenges associated with your investigations.

Exercise caution, particularly when handling sensitive subjects or topics, and be prepared to adapt your strategies to address unexpected obstacles.

In summary, SEON's advanced features and capabilities are invaluable assets for expert-level OSINT practitioners.

Mastering advanced search queries, custom alerts, data enrichment, and integration with external tools allows you to conduct in-depth investigations with precision.

However, ethical considerations and responsible use of the tool should always guide your actions.

Maintaining respect for privacy, legal compliance, and data verification are fundamental principles of conducting OSINT investigations at an advanced level.

With a deep understanding of SEON's advanced features and a commitment to ethical conduct, you can unlock the full potential of the tool and extract actionable intelligence, contributing significantly to your investigative objectives.

In the realm of open-source intelligence (OSINT), becoming an expert requires not only proficiency in using tools like SEON but also the strategic utilization of its advanced features and capabilities.

SEON is a powerful OSINT tool known for its versatility and depth, making it a crucial asset for those seeking to harness its power at an expert level.

To become an OSINT expert with SEON, one must develop a strategic mindset that combines technical proficiency with a deep understanding of intelligence gathering.

One of the key expert strategies in harnessing SEON's power is to establish clear objectives before conducting any investigation.

Define your goals, the type of information you seek, and the scope of your inquiry to ensure that your efforts are focused and targeted.

By setting well-defined objectives, you can maximize the efficiency of your SEON searches and extract relevant intelligence more effectively.

Additionally, as an expert OSINT practitioner, it's essential to master the art of crafting advanced search queries within SEON.

Utilize operators, filters, and Boolean logic to create precise search queries that sift through vast amounts of data and deliver highly relevant results.

This skill is invaluable for conducting in-depth investigations that yield actionable intelligence.

Customization is another expert strategy when using SEON.

Leverage SEON's advanced customization options to tailor your searches to the specific needs of your investigation.

Customize alerts, data enrichment settings, and notification preferences to create a workflow that aligns seamlessly with your objectives.

Furthermore, an expert OSINT practitioner understands the importance of continuous monitoring.

Set up custom alerts within SEON to receive real-time notifications when new information related to your subjects becomes available.

This proactive approach ensures that you stay updated on developments as they happen, allowing you to respond swiftly to emerging intelligence.

Advanced data enrichment is a feature that experts fully utilize within SEON.

By enriching collected data with additional information from various sources, you can create a more comprehensive and detailed profile of your subjects.

This depth of insight enhances your analytical capabilities and enables you to make more informed decisions.

Integration is a powerful strategy in SEON.

Connect SEON with other OSINT tools, data analysis platforms, or external databases to expand your investigative reach.

Integrating additional resources allows you to access a broader range of data sources and analytical tools, amplifying the depth and breadth of your intelligence gathering.

While harnessing SEON's power, ethical considerations should always be at the forefront.

Responsible and ethical conduct is non-negotiable in the world of OSINT.

Adhere to legal regulations, respect individual privacy, and ensure that your investigations remain within ethical boundaries.

In-depth verification of the accuracy and authenticity of the information you obtain through SEON is paramount.

Cross-reference and validate data from multiple sources to ensure that the intelligence you gather is reliable and trustworthy.

As an expert OSINT practitioner, it's crucial to adapt your strategies to address challenges and unforeseen obstacles.

OSINT investigations can be complex, and your ability to navigate these challenges with resilience and adaptability sets you apart as an expert.

In summary, expert strategies for harnessing SEON's power encompass a combination of technical proficiency, customization, and ethical conduct.

Establish clear objectives, craft advanced search queries, customize your SEON settings, and utilize data enrichment and integration to elevate your intelligence gathering capabilities.

Maintain a commitment to ethical conduct, privacy, and data verification throughout your investigations.

By incorporating these expert strategies, you can unlock the full potential of SEON and become an OSINT expert capable of extracting valuable intelligence and making a meaningful impact in your investigative pursuits.

Chapter 6: Lampyre's Hidden Potentials: Expert Insights

In the world of open-source intelligence (OSINT), Lampyre stands out as a tool renowned for its advanced data analysis techniques, and mastering these techniques is crucial for extracting valuable insights from diverse data sources.

To unlock Lampyre's advanced data analysis techniques, one must delve into its capabilities and develop a strategic approach to intelligence gathering.

Lampyre offers a range of advanced features and functions that allow OSINT practitioners to perform in-depth analysis and uncover hidden connections within data.

One of the fundamental strategies when using Lampyre at an advanced level is to understand the tool's interface and functionalities thoroughly.

Familiarize yourself with Lampyre's user-friendly interface, which provides access to a wide array of data analysis tools and modules.

This interface is designed to streamline the process of collecting, analyzing, and visualizing data, making it essential for expert-level OSINT work.

As you delve into Lampyre's advanced data analysis techniques, it's important to start with a clear objective.

Define the specific insights you aim to gain from your data analysis, as this will guide your approach and help you select the appropriate tools and modules within Lampyre.

Lampyre allows you to import data from various sources, including databases, social media, and web scraping, offering versatility that is invaluable for advanced OSINT investigations.

Advanced data analysis often involves dealing with large datasets, so developing proficiency in data manipulation and cleaning is essential.

Lampyre provides tools for data transformation, cleansing, and filtering, enabling you to prepare your data for meaningful analysis.

One of the key features in Lampyre is its ability to perform link analysis, which is a crucial technique for expert OSINT practitioners.

Link analysis allows you to identify connections and relationships within data, uncovering hidden patterns, and potentially exposing important leads or associations.

Advanced data visualization is another area where Lampyre excels.

Lampyre provides a range of visualization options, including charts, graphs, and network diagrams, to help you present your findings in a clear and comprehensible manner.

As an expert OSINT practitioner, you should explore these visualization tools to convey complex information effectively.

Lampyre also supports the integration of external data analysis tools and libraries, which is a strategy that experts can leverage to enhance their capabilities.

Integrating additional resources can extend the range of analytical techniques available to you and further deepen your data analysis.

While using Lampyre's advanced data analysis techniques, ethical considerations should always guide your actions.

Respect individual privacy, adhere to legal regulations, and ensure that your data analysis remains within ethical boundaries.

Furthermore, as you extract insights from your analysis, it's crucial to verify the accuracy and reliability of the information you uncover.

Cross-reference and validate data from multiple sources to confirm its authenticity.

Another advanced technique in Lampyre is entity recognition, which involves identifying and extracting specific entities such as names, locations, and organizations from unstructured text.

This technique can be highly valuable for OSINT investigations, especially when dealing with vast amounts of textual data.

Additionally, Lampyre's advanced data analysis techniques can be complemented by machine learning and natural language processing (NLP) tools.

These techniques enable you to automate the analysis of text data, extract sentiment analysis, and classify text according to predefined categories.

Machine learning and NLP can significantly enhance your ability to process and understand large volumes of textual information.

As you advance in your OSINT journey with Lampyre, it's essential to remain adaptable and responsive to challenges.

OSINT investigations can be complex, and expert practitioners are known for their ability to navigate these challenges effectively.

In summary, unlocking Lampyre's advanced data analysis techniques involves a combination of technical proficiency, strategic planning, and ethical conduct.

Familiarize yourself with Lampyre's interface, define clear objectives for your analysis, and develop proficiency in data manipulation and cleaning.

Explore link analysis, data visualization, and entity recognition to extract valuable insights, and consider integrating external tools and libraries for advanced analysis.

Always uphold ethical principles, respect privacy, and verify the accuracy of your findings.

By incorporating these strategies, you can unlock the full potential of Lampyre's advanced data analysis techniques and become an expert OSINT practitioner capable of extracting valuable intelligence from diverse data sources.

In the realm of open-source intelligence (OSINT), becoming an expert Lampyre user entails mastering advanced tips and techniques that go beyond the basics of the tool.

Lampyre is a powerful OSINT software known for its advanced data analysis capabilities, making it a valuable asset for expert practitioners seeking to extract actionable intelligence.

To harness Lampyre's full potential, it's essential to dive deep into its features and functionalities.

Begin by gaining a thorough understanding of Lampyre's user interface, as it serves as the gateway to a wide range of advanced data analysis tools and modules.

This user-friendly interface simplifies the process of collecting, analyzing, and visualizing data, enabling expert-level OSINT work.

As you embark on your journey to becoming an expert Lampyre user, it's crucial to start with a clear objective.

Define the specific insights you intend to derive from your data analysis, as this will guide your approach and help you select the appropriate tools and modules within Lampyre.

Lampyre offers the flexibility to import data from various sources, including databases, social media platforms, and web scraping, providing expert OSINT practitioners with a versatile toolkit.

Advanced data analysis often involves working with substantial datasets, necessitating proficiency in data manipulation and cleaning.

Lampyre provides tools for data transformation, cleansing, and filtering, allowing you to prepare your data for meaningful analysis.

One of the standout features of Lampyre is its link analysis capabilities, a fundamental technique for expert OSINT practitioners.

Link analysis enables you to uncover connections and relationships within data, unveiling hidden patterns and potentially revealing critical leads or associations.

Advanced data visualization is another area where Lampyre shines.

The software offers a range of visualization options, including charts, graphs, and network diagrams, facilitating the effective presentation of complex information.

As an expert OSINT practitioner, you should explore these visualization tools to convey your findings clearly and comprehensibly.

Lampyre also supports the integration of external data analysis tools and libraries, a strategy that experts can leverage to enhance their capabilities.

Integrating additional resources can expand the range of analytical techniques at your disposal and deepen your data analysis.

Ethical considerations should always guide your actions when using Lampyre's advanced data analysis techniques.

Respect for individual privacy, adherence to legal regulations, and the maintenance of ethical boundaries are essential principles.

Furthermore, as you extract insights from your analysis, it's crucial to verify the accuracy and reliability of the information you uncover.

Cross-reference and validate data from multiple sources to confirm its authenticity.

Entity recognition is another advanced technique available in Lampyre, involving the identification and extraction of specific entities such as names, locations, and organizations from unstructured text.

This technique can be highly valuable for OSINT investigations, particularly when dealing with extensive textual data.

Lampyre's advanced data analysis techniques can be complemented by machine learning and natural language processing (NLP) tools.

These techniques enable you to automate the analysis of text data, perform sentiment analysis, and classify text into predefined categories.

Machine learning and NLP can significantly enhance your ability to process and understand large volumes of textual information.

Adaptability and responsiveness to challenges are qualities that define expert OSINT practitioners.

OSINT investigations can be intricate, and experts are known for their ability to navigate these challenges effectively.

In summary, expert tips and techniques for Lampyre users encompass a blend of technical proficiency, strategic planning, and ethical conduct.

Familiarize yourself with Lampyre's interface, set clear objectives for your analysis, and develop data manipulation and cleaning skills.

Explore link analysis, data visualization, and entity recognition for extracting valuable insights.

Consider integrating external tools and libraries for advanced analysis.

Always uphold ethical principles, respect privacy, and verify the accuracy of your findings.

By incorporating these strategies, you can become an expert Lampyre user capable of harnessing its advanced data analysis capabilities and extracting actionable intelligence in the field of open-source intelligence.

Chapter 7: Data Analysis and Visualization: Expert Approaches

In the world of open-source intelligence (OSINT), expert data analysis methods are the key to extracting meaningful insights from a vast sea of information.

OSINT professionals, at the expert level, require a deep understanding of advanced data analysis techniques to navigate complex datasets effectively.

These methods go beyond the basics and involve a combination of technical expertise, critical thinking, and creativity.

To become proficient in expert data analysis for OSINT, it's essential to start with a solid foundation in data collection and management.

Experts know how to efficiently gather data from various sources, including social media platforms, websites, and databases.

They understand the importance of data quality, accuracy, and relevance, ensuring that the information they collect is reliable.

Once the data is collected, experts employ data preprocessing techniques to clean and prepare it for analysis.

This involves tasks such as data cleansing, transformation, and normalization, which are crucial for accurate analysis.

Advanced data analysis often requires experts to work with large datasets. They are skilled in handling big data and have the necessary tools and techniques at their disposal.

Experts are proficient in data manipulation, aggregation, and filtering, enabling them to extract valuable patterns and trends.

One of the hallmarks of expert data analysis in OSINT is the ability to perform complex link analysis.

This technique involves uncovering connections and relationships within the data, which can reveal hidden insights and critical leads.

Experts use link analysis to map out networks, identify key nodes, and understand the flow of information.

Visualization is a powerful tool in expert data analysis. OSINT professionals at this level are adept at creating visually appealing and informative graphs, charts, and diagrams.

Visualization not only makes complex data more accessible but also aids in conveying findings to stakeholders effectively.

Machine learning and artificial intelligence (AI) are integral to expert data analysis methods in OSINT.

Experts leverage these technologies to automate tasks such as data classification, sentiment analysis, and anomaly detection.

Machine learning algorithms can identify patterns and anomalies in data that may be challenging to detect manually.

Furthermore, experts in OSINT employ natural language processing (NLP) techniques to extract valuable insights from textual data.

NLP enables the analysis of unstructured text, including social media posts, news articles, and forum discussions.

Sentiment analysis, topic modeling, and entity recognition are some of the NLP methods used by experts to gain a deeper understanding of textual data.

Expert data analysts in OSINT also rely on geospatial analysis to uncover location-based insights.

They use geospatial data to map out the physical locations associated with individuals, organizations, or events.

This technique can be invaluable in tracking movements, identifying hotspots, and understanding the geographic context of an investigation.

As experts dive deeper into their data analysis, they often employ statistical analysis techniques.

These methods allow for hypothesis testing, regression analysis, and the exploration of correlations and dependencies within the data.

Statistical analysis helps experts validate their findings and draw meaningful conclusions.

Furthermore, experts in OSINT are skilled in the art of data storytelling. They can weave narratives from their analysis, presenting insights in a compelling and coherent manner.

This ability to tell a data-driven story is essential for conveying findings to decision-makers and stakeholders effectively.

Ethical considerations remain at the forefront of expert data analysis in OSINT. Experts adhere to strict ethical guidelines, respecting privacy, legal regulations, and ethical boundaries.

They understand the importance of responsible data handling and ensure that their analysis does not infringe on individuals' rights.

Validation and verification of data are paramount for experts. They cross-reference information from multiple sources to ensure its accuracy and reliability.

In summary, expert data analysis methods for OSINT professionals encompass a wide range of techniques and skills.

These experts possess a deep understanding of data collection, preprocessing, and manipulation.

They are proficient in advanced data analysis techniques such as link analysis, geospatial analysis, machine learning, and NLP.

Ethical considerations and responsible data handling are integral to their work.

With a solid foundation in these methods, expert OSINT professionals can extract valuable insights and provide critical intelligence in various domains, from security and law enforcement to business and academia.

In the realm of advanced data analysis, visualization techniques play a pivotal role in extracting in-depth insights and uncovering hidden patterns.

Advanced visualization methods go beyond basic charts and graphs, offering a deeper understanding of complex datasets.

OSINT professionals who are well-versed in these techniques can transform data into actionable intelligence.

One of the most powerful tools in the advanced visualization arsenal is interactive dashboards.

These dynamic interfaces allow users to explore data in real-time, drilling down into specific details and adjusting parameters on the fly.

Interactive dashboards are invaluable for decision-makers who need to make sense of vast amounts of information quickly.

Time-series analysis is another advanced visualization technique that helps uncover trends and patterns over time.

OSINT experts can use time-series visualizations to track changes in data, identify anomalies, and predict future developments.

Heatmaps are a favorite among advanced analysts for their ability to highlight density and concentration within datasets.

These visualizations use color gradients to represent data points' values, making it easy to spot clusters and outliers.

Network diagrams are indispensable for experts dealing with interconnected data, such as social networks or organizational structures.

These visualizations reveal relationships, hierarchies, and the flow of information between nodes, shedding light on complex networks.

Chord diagrams, a specific type of network visualization, excel at illustrating connections between entities or elements in a dataset.

They are particularly useful when exploring relationships between multiple variables simultaneously.

Sankey diagrams offer a unique way to visualize the flow of resources, such as money, energy, or information, through a system.

They help experts identify inefficiencies and pinpoint areas where optimization is needed.

Tree maps provide a hierarchical view of data, breaking it down into nested rectangles.

These visualizations are excellent for representing data with multiple levels of categorization, such as file systems or organizational structures.

Parallel coordinate plots are advanced visualizations that display multivariate data by using parallel axes to represent variables.

This technique helps experts identify patterns and correlations among different attributes within a dataset.

Word clouds are a popular choice for visualizing textual data, highlighting the most frequently occurring words in a document or dataset. They provide a quick overview of key terms and themes. Advanced data analysts also employ geospatial visualizations to gain insights from location-based data. Heatmaps, choropleth maps, and 3D globe visualizations are examples of geospatial techniques that help experts understand the geographic distribution of information. Hierarchical edge bundling is a sophisticated network visualization method that simplifies complex network structures.

It groups related nodes and edges together, making it easier to interpret intricate relationships. Advanced visualization tools often include support for augmented reality (AR) and virtual reality (VR), allowing experts to immerse themselves in data environments.

AR and VR can provide a unique perspective on data, enabling experts to explore 3D visualizations and gain a deeper understanding of spatial relationships.

Incorporating machine learning into visualization is a cutting-edge trend in advanced data analysis. Machine learning algorithms can automatically generate visualizations that reveal patterns and anomalies within data.

Augmented data storytelling is an emerging technique that combines data visualization with storytelling elements. Experts can use augmented data storytelling to guide viewers through complex datasets, providing context and insights along the way.

When utilizing advanced visualization techniques, it's crucial to consider the audience.

Experts must tailor their visualizations to the specific needs and preferences of stakeholders, ensuring that the insights are communicated effectively.

Furthermore, accessibility and interactivity should be key considerations in advanced data visualization.

Ensuring that visualizations are accessible to all users, including those with disabilities, is essential.

Interactivity allows stakeholders to engage with the data, empowering them to explore and extract their insights.

To summarize, advanced visualization techniques are a cornerstone of in-depth data analysis in the field of OSINT.

These methods offer powerful ways to uncover patterns, relationships, and insights within complex datasets.

From interactive dashboards to geospatial visualizations and augmented data storytelling, experts in OSINT have a wide array of tools at their disposal.

Tailoring visualizations to the audience and considering accessibility and interactivity are critical aspects of effective data communication.

With these advanced techniques, OSINT professionals can transform raw data into actionable intelligence, making informed decisions and contributing to their organizations' success.

Chapter 8: Legal and Ethical Challenges for OSINT Experts

Navigating the complex legal and ethical landscape in the world of Open-Source Intelligence (OSINT) is an essential aspect of conducting responsible and lawful investigations.

OSINT practitioners must operate within legal boundaries and adhere to ethical principles to maintain trust and credibility.

One of the primary legal considerations in OSINT is compliance with data protection laws and regulations.

These laws vary by jurisdiction but generally govern the collection, processing, and storage of personal information.

OSINT professionals must be aware of the specific regulations in their area of operation and ensure they are not violating individuals' privacy rights.

In addition to data protection laws, copyright and intellectual property rights must also be considered when gathering and sharing information.

Using copyrighted material without permission or proper attribution can lead to legal consequences.

Ethical considerations in OSINT encompass a broader range of principles and guidelines that go beyond legal obligations.

One of the key ethical principles is respecting individuals' privacy and consent.

OSINT practitioners should only collect information from publicly available sources or sources where consent has been granted.

Using deceptive or intrusive methods to obtain information is generally considered unethical.

Transparency is another fundamental ethical principle in OSINT.

Practitioners should be transparent about their intentions and identity when conducting investigations.

Misrepresenting oneself or one's purpose can harm both the practitioner's reputation and the credibility of the information gathered.

OSINT professionals should always strive to provide accurate and reliable information.

Misinformation or inaccurate data can have significant consequences, especially in critical decision-making processes.

Verifying information from multiple sources and using reputable sources is crucial.

In the age of social media and online communities, OSINT practitioners must also be mindful of online harassment and cyberbullying.

Engaging in aggressive or harmful behavior toward individuals online is not only unethical but can also lead to legal repercussions.

Respect for the boundaries of public and private information is another ethical consideration.

Practitioners should refrain from delving into individuals' private lives or using OSINT techniques to harass or harm them.

Ensuring that the benefits of OSINT outweigh any potential harm is a constant ethical challenge.

OSINT professionals should weigh the potential consequences of their actions and make informed decisions about whether to proceed with an investigation. In some cases, OSINT practitioners may encounter sensitive or classified information.

Handling such information requires the utmost discretion and adherence to legal and ethical guidelines.

Sharing or disseminating sensitive information without proper authorization can result in severe legal consequences.

Maintaining confidentiality and safeguarding sources is also essential.

OSINT practitioners should take steps to protect their sources and prevent them from facing harm or retaliation.

Additionally, OSINT professionals should be aware of the evolving nature of technology and its impact on privacy and ethics.

New tools and techniques may raise novel ethical questions, requiring practitioners to adapt and stay informed.

Ultimately, OSINT practitioners must strike a delicate balance between their investigative goals, legal responsibilities, and ethical principles.

This balance ensures that they operate with integrity and responsibility while harnessing the power of OSINT for legitimate purposes.

It is crucial for practitioners to stay updated on legal developments and ethical standards in their field and seek guidance when faced with complex legal and ethical dilemmas.

In summary, navigating the complex legal and ethical issues in OSINT is a critical aspect of responsible and effective intelligence gathering.

Practitioners must adhere to data protection laws, respect privacy rights, and follow ethical principles such as transparency, accuracy, and respect for boundaries.

Balancing investigative goals with legal and ethical responsibilities ensures the integrity and credibility of OSINT operations.

Continuous learning and staying informed about evolving technology and regulations are essential for OSINT professionals to navigate this intricate landscape successfully.

Maintaining ethical integrity as an expert in any field, including Open-Source Intelligence (OSINT), is of paramount importance to preserve credibility and trust.

It involves adhering to a set of ethical principles and best practices that guide your conduct in all professional endeavors.

One of the foundational principles of ethical integrity is honesty.

Being truthful and transparent in all your actions and communications is essential.

This means not misrepresenting information, concealing facts, or engaging in deceptive practices.

Honesty builds trust with colleagues, clients, and the public.

Another crucial aspect of ethical integrity is respecting the privacy and consent of individuals.

In the world of OSINT, it's common to gather information from publicly available sources, but it's equally important to ensure that you are not invading someone's privacy.

Always obtain consent when necessary and avoid intruding into someone's personal life.

Transparency is a key practice in maintaining ethical integrity.

Be open about your intentions, methodologies, and affiliations when conducting investigations.

This transparency helps build trust and credibility with those you interact with.

Respecting the boundaries of public and private information is an ethical guideline that OSINT experts must follow.

Avoid delving into individuals' private lives or using information gathered in a harmful or intrusive manner.

Ethical integrity also extends to the responsible handling of sensitive or classified information.

Practicing discretion and safeguarding confidential data is essential to prevent harm and legal consequences.

Verifying information is a crucial practice to ensure accuracy and ethical integrity.

Avoid spreading unverified or false information, as it can have significant repercussions.

Always verify information from multiple reliable sources before considering it as accurate.

Avoiding conflicts of interest is another important ethical practice.

Ensure that your professional and personal interests do not compromise the objectivity of your investigations.

Transparency about any potential conflicts is essential to maintain ethical integrity.

Professionalism is integral to ethical integrity.

Treat colleagues, clients, and subjects of your investigations with respect and courtesy.

Unprofessional behavior can tarnish your reputation and damage relationships.

In the rapidly evolving field of OSINT, continuous learning and staying updated on ethical standards and legal regulations are essential.

Keep abreast of changes in technology, data privacy laws, and ethical guidelines to adapt your practices accordingly.

Ethical integrity also involves seeking guidance and advice when faced with complex ethical dilemmas.

Consulting with peers or ethics committees can provide valuable insights and ensure you make ethically sound decisions.

OSINT experts should always prioritize the protection of their sources.

Safeguarding the identities and information of sources is essential to prevent them from facing harm or retaliation.

Remember that ethical integrity is not only about adhering to the letter of the law but also about upholding the spirit of ethical principles.

It's about doing what is right and just, even when there are no specific legal obligations.

Ethical decision-making often involves weighing potential harm against the benefits of an action.

Consider the consequences of your actions carefully and make informed decisions.

In summary, maintaining ethical integrity as an expert in OSINT requires a commitment to honesty, transparency, privacy, and responsible conduct.

Following these best practices ensures that you uphold the highest ethical standards in your field.

Ethical integrity not only preserves your reputation but also contributes to the credibility and trustworthiness of the entire OSINT community.

Continuous learning, professionalism, and ethical reflection are key components of maintaining ethical integrity in this dynamic field.

Chapter 9: Expert OSINT Case Studies and Challenges

Analyzing expert-level OSINT case studies offers invaluable insights into the practical application of Open-Source Intelligence techniques in real-world scenarios.

These case studies provide a glimpse into how OSINT experts leverage their knowledge and tools to solve complex problems, uncover critical information, and contribute to various fields.

One common theme in expert-level OSINT case studies is the thorough understanding of the subject matter.

OSINT experts often specialize in specific domains, such as cybersecurity, law enforcement, or corporate investigations, and their in-depth knowledge is a crucial asset.

In many cases, expert OSINT practitioners are called upon to solve intricate cybersecurity challenges.

They might investigate cyber threats, track down malicious actors, or assess vulnerabilities in digital infrastructures.

In these cases, their ability to analyze online data and trace digital footprints is instrumental in identifying threats and devising effective countermeasures.

Expert OSINT practitioners are also frequently involved in legal investigations.

They may assist law enforcement agencies, attorneys, or private investigators in gathering evidence for criminal or civil cases.

Their expertise in locating and validating online information can be pivotal in building a solid case or uncovering critical facts.

Furthermore, OSINT experts often play a vital role in due diligence processes for businesses and corporations.

Before entering into partnerships or investments, companies rely on OSINT specialists to conduct thorough background checks on potential collaborators or competitors.

Expert-level OSINT practitioners can uncover hidden risks, financial irregularities, or other critical factors that may influence business decisions.

One key aspect of expert-level OSINT work is the ability to navigate the deep web and dark web.

These hidden corners of the internet are home to various illegal activities, including cybercrime, black market trading, and extremist content.

OSINT experts are trained to access and monitor these areas while complying with legal and ethical standards.

By infiltrating these hidden online communities, they can gather intelligence on threats, criminal activities, or extremist ideologies.

Social media platforms, with their vast user bases and wealth of user-generated content, are another area where OSINT experts excel.

They can track individuals or groups across different platforms, analyze their online behaviors, and identify potential risks or opportunities.

This capability is particularly valuable for tracking down missing persons, monitoring extremist movements, or conducting online reputation management.

In the realm of geopolitics and international relations, OSINT experts contribute to the analysis of global events.

They monitor news, social media, and publicly available information to assess the political, economic, and social landscapes of various countries.

Their insights can help governments, think tanks, and organizations make informed decisions and anticipate potential developments.

Expert-level OSINT practitioners also excel in the field of competitive intelligence.

They help businesses gather information on their competitors, market trends, and emerging technologies.

By analyzing publicly available data, they can provide valuable strategic insights to help companies stay ahead in their industries.

In the context of threat intelligence, OSINT experts monitor and analyze online chatter and activities to identify potential security threats.

They can detect early signs of cyberattacks, hacktivist campaigns, or other malicious activities and provide organizations with actionable intelligence to enhance their cybersecurity measures.

Additionally, expert-level OSINT practitioners often work on humanitarian projects.

They help locate missing persons, track disease outbreaks, or assess the impact of natural disasters by analyzing publicly available data and collaborating with relevant organizations.

The work of OSINT experts can be critical in saving lives and providing timely assistance in humanitarian crises.

When analyzing expert-level OSINT case studies, it becomes evident that the field is continuously evolving.

New tools, technologies, and data sources emerge, requiring OSINT experts to adapt and expand their skillsets continually.

Moreover, the ethical considerations and legal boundaries of OSINT are constantly evolving, challenging practitioners to stay compliant and uphold ethical standards.

In summary, analyzing expert-level OSINT case studies showcases the versatility and significance of Open-Source Intelligence in various domains.

From cybersecurity to law enforcement, from business intelligence to geopolitics, OSINT experts play a crucial role in gathering, analyzing, and disseminating actionable information.

Their work contributes to informed decision-making, enhances security, and supports humanitarian efforts in an ever-changing world.

Tackling complex OSINT challenges at an expert level requires a deep understanding of both the techniques and the subject matter.

Expert OSINT practitioners often deal with cases that involve multifaceted issues, elusive targets, or vast amounts of data.

One of the primary challenges in complex OSINT operations is the sheer volume of information available on the internet.

Experts must sift through this vast sea of data to find relevant and actionable intelligence.

To do this effectively, they employ advanced search strategies and filtering techniques.

Another challenge is the credibility and authenticity of online information.

In the age of misinformation and fake news, OSINT experts must critically evaluate sources and cross-reference information to ensure its accuracy.

Dealing with information overload is a common hurdle in complex OSINT investigations.

Experts use data analysis tools and visualization techniques to make sense of large datasets and identify patterns, trends, or anomalies.

In some cases, they might need to correlate data from various sources to build a comprehensive picture.

A significant aspect of tackling complex OSINT challenges is the ability to adapt to evolving technologies and platforms.

New social media platforms, communication channels, and data sources constantly emerge, and experts must stay updated to remain effective.

Staying anonymous and protecting one's identity is crucial when conducting sensitive OSINT investigations.

Experts employ various techniques to maintain their privacy and security, such as using VPNs, anonymous browsing, and secure communication channels.

Complex OSINT investigations often involve open-source intelligence fusion.

This means integrating OSINT data with other forms of intelligence, such as human intelligence (HUMINT) or signals intelligence (SIGINT), to create a more comprehensive intelligence picture.

Experts with experience in multiple intelligence disciplines excel in this aspect.

Understanding the legal and ethical boundaries is paramount in complex OSINT operations.

Experts are well-versed in the legal requirements and ethical considerations relevant to their field, ensuring that their actions remain within the boundaries of the law.

Dealing with encryption and secure communication presents challenges in modern OSINT operations.

Experts may encounter encrypted messages or data that require advanced decryption techniques to access.

Maintaining a high level of discretion and operational security (OPSEC) is vital to prevent targets from becoming aware of the investigation.

Experts are cautious about leaving digital footprints that could compromise their anonymity or the integrity of their investigations.

Complex OSINT challenges often involve dealing with international aspects.

Experts might need to navigate foreign languages, cultures, and online communities to gather intelligence.

Cultural sensitivity and language skills can be assets in these situations.

In some cases, experts must work with limited information or incomplete data.

This requires them to employ creative thinking and inference to fill in the gaps and make informed assessments.

OSINT experts are skilled at triangulating information from multiple sources to confirm its accuracy and reliability.

Advanced data analysis techniques, such as network analysis or sentiment analysis, are commonly used by experts to extract valuable insights from unstructured data.

Collaboration and information sharing are essential in complex OSINT challenges.

Experts often work in teams or collaborate with experts from other fields to leverage their collective knowledge and skills.

Advanced OSINT practitioners also focus on operational security (OPSEC) and counterintelligence.

They are aware of potential adversaries or threats to their investigations and take precautions to safeguard their operations.

When tackling complex OSINT challenges, experts understand the importance of documenting their findings and methodologies.

Clear and comprehensive documentation is critical for reporting and presenting findings to clients, law enforcement, or other stakeholders.

Ultimately, the success of complex OSINT operations depends on the expertise, experience, and resourcefulness of the practitioners involved.

These experts possess a combination of technical skills, critical thinking, and domain knowledge that allows them to tackle even the most intricate OSINT challenges successfully.

Chapter 10: Achieving Mastery: Expert Commando Stories and Takeaways

Stories and insights from expert OSINT commandos provide valuable lessons and inspiration for those in the field.

These individuals have honed their skills over years of experience, often facing complex challenges and navigating the ever-changing landscape of open-source intelligence.

Their stories highlight the importance of adaptability and continuous learning in the world of OSINT.

One common theme in the narratives of expert OSINT commandos is the evolution of their careers.

Many started as novices, learning the basics of OSINT and gradually building their expertise through practice and perseverance.

They share their journeys to help others understand that becoming an expert in OSINT is a gradual process, requiring dedication and commitment.

Expert OSINT practitioners often emphasize the need for a strong foundation in the fundamentals.

These commandos stress that mastering the basics of OSINT tools and techniques is essential before diving into more advanced operations.

They share how they spent countless hours honing their skills in areas like data analysis, online research, and tool usage.

Expert OSINT commandos also frequently discuss the value of mentorship and collaboration.

They recount stories of working with seasoned professionals who guided them, shared insights, and provided opportunities for growth.

These partnerships often played a pivotal role in their development as experts in the field.

One common challenge faced by expert OSINT practitioners is the ethical dilemma of their work.

They share stories of navigating the fine line between conducting legal and ethical investigations and potentially crossing into unethical territory.

These anecdotes serve as cautionary tales and remind others in the field of the importance of maintaining ethical integrity.

Expert OSINT commandos are often called upon to tackle high-stakes cases and investigations.

They recount experiences where their expertise led to critical breakthroughs, helping law enforcement agencies solve crimes or uncover valuable intelligence.

These success stories highlight the tangible impact that OSINT can have on real-world situations.

In addition to their success stories, expert OSINT practitioners also share their failures and setbacks.

These narratives emphasize that even the most experienced commandos encounter challenges and make mistakes.

However, they stress the importance of learning from these failures and using them as opportunities for growth.

Expert OSINT commandos often reflect on the rapid evolution of technology and its impact on their work.

They discuss how the emergence of new platforms, social media trends, and communication tools constantly reshapes the OSINT landscape.

Adaptability and staying up-to-date with emerging technologies are key themes in their stories.

Another recurring theme in their narratives is the critical role of data analysis and visualization.

Expert commandos share how their advanced data analysis skills allowed them to uncover hidden patterns, connections, and insights within vast amounts of information.

They stress the importance of mastering data analysis techniques for success in OSINT.

The experiences of expert OSINT commandos also shed light on the international aspects of their work.

They recount stories of cross-border investigations, language barriers, and the challenges of navigating foreign online communities.

These narratives showcase the global reach and impact of OSINT operations.

Ultimately, the stories and insights from expert OSINT commandos offer a comprehensive view of the field.

They provide guidance for aspiring practitioners, highlighting the importance of continuous learning, ethical conduct, adaptability, and collaboration.

These narratives serve as a testament to the dedication and expertise of those who have mastered the art of open-source intelligence.

Aspiring OSINT experts can derive several key takeaways from the experiences and insights of those who have already excelled in the field.

First and foremost, building a strong foundation in the fundamentals of OSINT is crucial.

This involves becoming proficient in using basic tools and techniques, understanding data sources, and developing research skills.

Novice practitioners should dedicate time to learning and mastering these fundamental aspects.

Mentorship and guidance play a pivotal role in one's journey to becoming an OSINT expert.

Seeking guidance from experienced professionals can accelerate the learning process and provide valuable insights.

Aspiring experts should actively seek opportunities to collaborate with and learn from seasoned practitioners.

Continuous learning is a recurring theme among OSINT experts.

The field is dynamic, with new tools, platforms, and techniques emerging regularly.

Therefore, staying up-to-date with the latest developments is essential for growth.

Experts emphasize the importance of ongoing training and self-education.

Ethical considerations are a cornerstone of OSINT practice.

Aspiring experts should prioritize ethical conduct in their work.

This includes respecting privacy, adhering to legal boundaries, and maintaining ethical integrity.

Navigating the ethical landscape of OSINT is a skill that should be honed from the beginning.

Failure is an inevitable part of the learning process in OSINT.

Aspiring experts should not be discouraged by setbacks or mistakes.

Instead, they should view these experiences as opportunities for improvement and growth.

Learning from failures is a critical aspect of becoming an expert.

Advanced data analysis and visualization are key skills for OSINT experts.

Aspiring practitioners should invest time in developing these capabilities.

These skills enable experts to extract meaningful insights from vast amounts of data, enhancing the value of their investigations.

Adaptability is a quality that OSINT experts value highly.

The field is ever-evolving, and practitioners must adapt to new technologies, platforms, and communication trends.

Aspiring experts should cultivate a mindset of adaptability to thrive in this dynamic environment.

Collaboration and teamwork are essential components of OSINT success.

Aspiring experts should actively seek opportunities to collaborate with others in the field.

Collaborative efforts often lead to a broader and more effective approach to OSINT investigations.

Effective communication is a skill that experts emphasize.

Clear and concise communication is crucial when presenting findings, working with clients, or collaborating with colleagues.

Aspiring experts should work on honing their communication skills to convey complex information effectively.

Global awareness is another important aspect of OSINT expertise.

The field extends beyond national borders, and practitioners may find themselves involved in international investigations.

Understanding cultural nuances and navigating foreign online communities are valuable skills for OSINT experts.

Experts in the field highlight the need for a strong work ethic and dedication.

OSINT investigations can be time-consuming and require meticulous attention to detail.

Aspiring experts should be prepared to put in the effort required for thorough research and analysis.

Finally, OSINT experts stress the importance of staying ethical and lawful in all endeavors.

Unethical or illegal actions can have severe consequences, both professionally and legally.

Aspiring experts should always operate within the boundaries of the law and maintain the highest ethical standards.

In summary, aspiring OSINT experts can learn valuable lessons from the experiences and wisdom of those who have already achieved expertise in the field.

Building a strong foundation, seeking mentorship, continuous learning, ethical conduct, adaptability, collaboration, effective communication, global awareness, work ethic, and legality are key takeaways that can guide their journey toward becoming proficient OSINT practitioners.

Top of Form

Conclusion

In this comprehensive book bundle, "OSINT Commando," we embarked on an exciting journey through the realm of Open-Source Intelligence (OSINT). Across four distinct volumes, we explored the intricate world of OSINT, from its foundational principles to the advanced strategies employed by elite practitioners. Our goal was to equip readers with the knowledge and skills necessary to become proficient OSINT operatives, capable of navigating the digital landscape, uncovering critical information, and operating ethically and legally.

In "Book 1 - OSINT Commando: A Comprehensive Guide for Beginners and Experts," we laid the groundwork for OSINT exploration. We covered the fundamental concepts, tools, and techniques, ensuring that both novices and experienced professionals had a solid foundation to build upon. With an emphasis on ethical conduct and responsible information gathering, we set the stage for a successful OSINT journey.

"Book 2 - From Novice to Ninja: Mastering OSINT Commando with Spokeo, Spiderfoot, SEON, and Lampyre" elevated our readers' skills to the next level. Here, we delved deep into the capabilities of four powerful OSINT tools: Spokeo, Spiderfoot, SEON, and Lampyre. Through comprehensive tutorials and real-world examples, we guided readers on a path from novice to mastery, enabling them to harness the full potential of these tools for advanced reconnaissance and intelligence gathering.

"Book 3 - OSINT Commando Unleashed: Taking Your Skills from Entry-Level to Elite" unveiled the secrets of elite OSINT practitioners. We explored advanced techniques, strategies, and methodologies used by the best in the field. By showcasing real-world case studies and challenging scenarios, we encouraged readers to push their boundaries and elevate their skills to an elite level.

Finally, "Book 4 - Expert Strategies in OSINT Commando: Unlocking Secrets at Every Skill Level" provided a masterclass in OSINT expertise. We revealed the expert-level strategies, insights, and tactics that can unlock the most well-guarded secrets. Through a collection of expert case studies and experiences, we shared the wisdom of those who have reached the pinnacle of OSINT excellence.

As we conclude this OSINT Commando book bundle, we want to emphasize that the journey in the world of OSINT is ongoing. It is a dynamic and evolving field, where learning never stops. We hope that the knowledge and skills imparted in these four volumes serve as a valuable resource for your continued growth and success in the realm of Open-Source Intelligence.

Remember that with great power comes great responsibility. Ethical conduct, legal compliance, and respect for privacy must always be at the forefront of your OSINT endeavors. As you venture forth as an OSINT Commando, may you use your newfound expertise to make informed decisions, solve complex problems, and contribute positively to the world of information and intelligence.

Thank you for embarking on this OSINT Commando journey with us, and we wish you the very best in your future OSINT endeavors. Stay curious, stay ethical, and stay vigilant. The world of OSINT awaits your exploration and discovery.

www.ingramcontent.com/pod-product-compliance
Lightning Source LLC
Chambersburg PA
CBHW071235050326
40690CB00011B/2132